EXPOSED

EILEEN CURTEIS

CCB Publishing
British Columbia, Canada

Exposed

Copyright ©2018 by Eileen Curteis
ISBN-13   978-1-77143-359-4
First Edition

Library and Archives Canada Cataloguing in Publication
Curteis, Eileen, 1942-, author
Exposed / written and illustrated by Eileen Curteis. -- First edition.
Issued in print and electronic formats.
ISBN 978-1-77143-359-4 (softcover).--ISBN 978-1-77143-360-0 (PDF)
Additional cataloguing data available from Library and Archives Canada

Cover artwork and interior pastel drawings, collages, watercolour paintings, as well as all poems and prose are by Eileen Curteis.

Cover design by Carey Pallister.

Author photo credit: Frances Litman – www.franceslitman.com

Extreme care has been taken by the author to ensure that all information presented in this book is accurate and up to date at the time of publishing. Neither the author nor the publisher can be held responsible for any errors or omissions. Additionally, neither is any liability assumed for damages resulting from the use of the information contained herein.

All rights reserved. No part of this publication may be reproduced, stored in a retrieval system or transmitted in any form or by any means, electronic, mechanical, photocopying, recording or otherwise without the express written permission of the publisher.

Publisher: CCB Publishing
              British Columbia, Canada
              www.ccbpublishing.com

The mouth

that whispers God

knows

where she came from.

Written for my friends

who travel the Journey with me.

<u>Acknowledgement</u>: Carey Pallister, Province Archivist for the Sisters of Saint Ann, deserves recognition for her editorial suggestions, digital skills and great generosity in helping me put this manuscript together.

CONTENTS

Introduction: The Call of the Artist and
Poet in Religious Life 7

Preface: Comments from the Archivist,
Carey Pallister 9

POETRY, PROSE, PASTEL, COLLAGE and
WATERCOLOUR ART

Openness 14
Simplicity 18
Fly 22
Humility 26
Paradox 30
Holy Rebellion 34
Ecstasy 38
Melancholy Joy 42
Girl Child Sings 46
Mountain Climber 50
Cocoon Breaker 54
Ocean Survivor 58
Sunrise 62
Fragility 66
Beloved Messenger 70
Serenity 74

Daybreak 78
Spider Woman 82
Woman Alive 86
Gentle Strum 90
Naked Love 94
Soul Fire 98
Risen One 102
Water Jug 106
Floating Free 110
Joyful Pilgrim 114
Isolate Beauty 118
Transfigured Misfit 122
Wind-Tossed Freedom 126
Cyclonic Lover 130
Cargo Lifter 134
New Vision 138
Seasoned Woman 142
Cross Carrier 146
Gracious Gardener 150
Healing Rainstorm 154
Gluttonous Love 158
Spiritual Rebirth 162
Night Watch 166
Inward Gaze 170
Message Carrier 174

Awakenment	178
Thorny Breakthrough	182
Quiet Triumph	186
Winter Bird	190
Shepherd of Nowhere	194
Prophetic Word	198
Eternal Waters	202
Sun Woman	206
Ascended Soul	210
Stillness	214
Foreign Dancer	218
Strongly Rooted	222
Gifted Orphan	226
Free Spirit	230
Closed Mouth Open	234
Victory	238
Doorway Through	242
Face of God	246

INTRODUCTION

THE CALL OF THE ARTIST AND POET IN RELIGIOUS LIFE

If loving God is my passion, which it is, then I would have to say that art and poetry is the stimulus behind it. For me, it began when I entered religious life at age nineteen. Nobody had told me about mysticism, but when I encountered it I knew I would be in love with Love forever. Fifty-seven years later it is no different. The mystical truth inside the human journey is what spurs me on to be a co-creator with God whether it be in my teaching, healing work or the literary arts.

My art flourished in the mid and late seventies, and my poetry has continued to the present day, into a kind of maturity I was not capable of in my younger years. I would describe myself as a visual artist without training. How the art happened still remains somewhat of a mystery to me. I would simply sit in quiet prayer and take a pencil or paint brush in hand. Suddenly a Love Force, which I call the Holy Spirit, would guide my hand and I would suddenly see the vision on paper. My soul energy was in the work and it gave me insight into the woman I was and would be becoming. Most of my earlier line drawings of forty-one years ago were done in pastel colours to match the feeling of my soul.

In the springtime of my year of hermitage, 1979-1980, the drawings that emerged were done in stark black and white. Somehow they seemed to carry the profundity of what my soul was feeling.

Through the years, only a small amount of my work was done in watercolour. Being a teacher of small children I simply used the same kind of paint box that the children I taught were using.

Today, I feel called to share with you a volume of work I have entitled, *Exposed*. In it, you will find my pastel drawings and watercolour art of forty-one years ago. With each drawing there is a poem and prose piece revealing how the creative Spirit has been my revelatory Teacher.

Eileen Curteis, ssa

PREFACE

COMMENTS FROM THE ARCHIVIST, CAREY PALLISTER

"The mouth that whispers God, knows where she came from" – Eileen Curteis

Inner Voice: My Voice
Without Voice: No Voice
Voices of Others: Their Voice
Voice of God: The Voice

How do you capture a life in words and how do you do it justice, especially when it was a long time ago, when you were someone else? You had not yet experienced life. You had not met those who would influence you positively and negatively. And in the future you would become someone else completely; physically, spiritually, mentally and emotionally.

Vulnerability, in essence, exposure of self, is our greatest fear and our greatest asset. With the passage of each stage of human development, we shed fragments of our protective shell until we are rendered insignificant and defenseless. Still, we are capable of maturing, flourishing and accomplishing so much; it is part of the complexity of the human journey.

As you navigate the paths of your life, you have no idea which words, encounters or divine guidance will spark an awakening in you. Your memories travel with you wherever you go and are waiting for you when you return, but sometimes your past can come crashing into your present when you least expect it and then you need to find your voice.

Nobody else has your voice, your journey, your memories, your story, your vision. It is up to you to influence, uplift and create joy or pain by using your voice. Touching the lives of others in meaningful and positive ways is one of the many powers of the voice.

The word *voice* is used in 432 Bible verses in 73 chapters in 45 books. A Google search of voice finds over a billion results. In essence, the word *voice* is significant, as is indeed are the actions of speaking, hearing and listening to someone else's voice; the divine voice within you, working deeply on a soul level.

We are living in a time when many voices that were previously silenced are now being heard;

Reconciliation – the voices of the First Nations; The #MeToo movement – the voices of mistreated women; Black Lives Matter – campaigns against violence and systemic racism toward black people and Never Again Movement - students for gun control so they can feel safe at school.

Anger, hurt and subjugation make us want to be heard, to rally against past wrongs, iniquity, hate and violence and we hope that by raising our voices it will lead to justice, peace and love. But sometimes it is our own life experience that we want to share; we want our voice to be heard.

We carry a lifetime of luggage; physical, spiritual, mental and emotional and each are accompanied by a voice: Inner Voice - my voice; Without Voice - no voice; Voices of Others - their voice and Voice of God - The Voice. We experience all these voices in us. They make us, guide us, warn us and console us.

The poems and prose in *Exposed* are an intimacy of words, contributions from the soul, a voice from long ago which has waited for a long time to be heard. This manuscript was

Divinely inspired and Divinely gifted. From childhood experiences of loneliness and isolation to healing and joy, love and hurt, *Exposed* is a courageous metaphoric work that will touch the reader deeply, addressing issues with which we can all identify.

Coming from a hierarchical ethos, where she struggled and often felt her diminishment, Eileen has now reclaimed her individuality and found her voice immersed within, while at the same time, being very present to the Religious Community she loves. Spontaneous and authentic, Eileen's work is a deep personal expression of past and present experiences, challenging her to become the person she is today.

From deep within this mystic, beautiful woman, appears a truth and an honesty that is unquestionably passionate and open. It flows onto the page with words and art. The words are recent, ascending from a place of healing; a gift from God that is unquestioned and received with joy and a sense of wonderment and fulfillment.

Created by the author more than forty years ago, the art in *Exposed* is unique, emotional and powerful, waiting for this moment to reveal its meaning; the two now are united in this book.

How do you capture a life in words? Only you truly know your heart, your essence and sometimes we need courage to find our voice to express it.

Written with love,
Carey Pallister

OPENNESS

Brutal judgement
can stab a person open
but not in the journal
of this woman's life.

She takes an axe to it
bursts open the stone
and crushes it.

A bent woman
lying on the ground
you need
to be patient with her.

It takes time
for a house to crumble
before it falls,
time for the hard wood
to become pliable.

And even more time
for the clay body
of a woman
to push open
the lid that closed it.

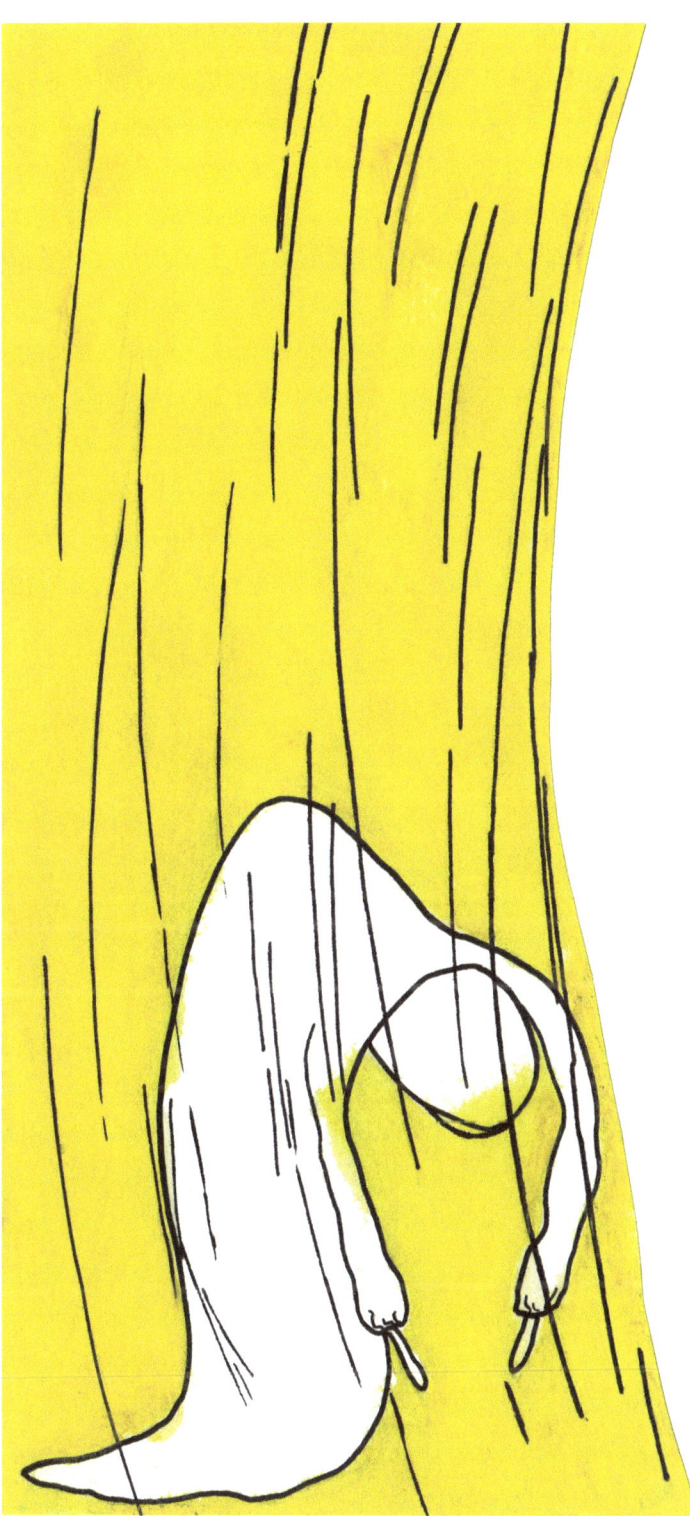

OPENNESS

In the beginning Openness was open. She had eyes to see and ears to hear. The air was pure where she lived and often you would see her drifting through the clouds as if she knew where she was going. She loved everyone and everything but most of all she adored her Creator.

One morning when she was bathing in the eternal waters everything shifted. There was an eerie sound overhead and she saw what she had never seen before. The smooth water had ruffles in it and the clouds that she so dearly clung to were falling earthward. Threatening grey streaks had already destroyed the beauty of her orange sun and the blue sky, bluer than blue, had lost its brilliance. Beside her a black heron stood stiller than still.

Openness had no bones or flesh to cover her and, yet, she could feel a shiver running through the body of her soul. "Where am I?" she said, and then came the Voice she knew so well. "I want you to plant a garden. It will be as small as you are but one day it will grow into a lush forest and I will be there to water it with you. Then and only then will you return to me. Go now and do as I say."

Openness was an obedient child and somehow knew her time had come. Descending like a parachute from the heavens she came swiftly, softly, quietly into the family that would welcome her. She was no different than any child other than being a girl child. People soon learned about her brightness and said she was so pure you couldn't find a blotch in her. At first, nothing seemed difficult. It was as if Openness could turn night into day, a stone into a star, an eclipse into a full moon and, yet, there was a side of this child that no one knew. Even though she was a sweet, sensitive soul with a heart that was soft as a moccasin, she would have to take off her shoes and learn the hard way.

As a young student learning never came easy. Sometimes her gypsy mind would wander out of the classroom into faraway places. She seemed to have a direct line with her Creator and even though this topic was not on the curriculum she had a way of keeping the conversation going. Concentration was not her best subject. In fact, she failed badly. What her teacher didn't know was that when you're in Love you're in love.

Being a Divine child, living in the real world was something Openness never quite got used to until the day when she became big. This time instead of dodging pain, she walked through it with the grace of a fine tuned athlete. More than anything she loved her new way of being and was quick to learn that people are like trees in a forest and that we are all here to help one another grow. Sinking her roots deep into the soil, she could feel the lush ground under her, and inside the bark of every tree she could hear these words: the mouth that whispers God knows where she came from.

SIMPLICITY

There's nothing complex
about the rain.
In a moment of scalding
she's the harmless one
shielding you from danger.

Living in a vacant world
of your own wounding
she sees above and beyond you.

Her Spirit is bigger than you are
and she breathes
with the breath
that is in you.

Tall as a tree and even taller
she's the soft drizzle
blowing in the wind
the Mother God
walking upright in you.

Uncomplicated as a wheel
spinning its way home
she seems to know the route
ahead of time.

SIMPLICITY

One day Simplicity wandered away from the tribe. "Enough is enough!" she said. "My days of pretending are over." On the outside Simplicity looked like everyone else but on the inside there was a chain holding her down. In order to become free she knew she needed to leave the homestead that she loved. Whether her going would be permanent or temporary would remain to be seen.

On the day of her departure she awoke early with the singing of a bird. It was as if a good omen had landed on her shoulder and she was given wings to fly. Something was urging her on, an unexplainable Something that was pushing her out of the nest. Soon she would be gone and no one would be there to stop her, not even the foliage on the tree she loved.

Some criticized her going with a harshness she didn't deserve. Others said, "She could have at least left a note," but for Simplicity it all happened so quickly and before she knew it the door had closed behind her. Rumours began spreading and sometimes the ripple of them reached Simplicity. Trying to defend herself was a useless task, no different than having your name erased from the good Book.

What Simplicity soon learned, was that aiming to please others was like falling off the jagged edge of a cliff. It never got her anywhere and it left her feeling dismal for days.

Even though people judged her behavior, leaving the tribe was the healthiest thing that ever happened. Simplicity needed to flow like a river and no one could do it for her. Through the years she had become a prisoner of her own isolation and without water for her soul she had grown into a desert of her own making.

Tired, restless and weary, she lay down with her brain beside her. "Stop thinking," she said. "Stop doing what you're doing. Go into that pool and be cleansed." It certainly wasn't easy. Anger never is. And, yet, each time she coughed up a negative thought the static in her brain would cease. It was like going through a sieve – smooth, cool, refreshing and, yet, sometimes the grit would stick to her.

At times like this, Simplicity could hardly bear the complexity of her journey and often wished the nightmare of it would be over. Sometimes she would be full of joy and whenever she wanted more of it an irresistible cloud of melancholy would swoop down over her. She soon learned that you don't teach endurance. You just endure.

Slowly, steadily, the healing took place. Winter turned into spring and suddenly, without warning, Simplicity stood on the verandah of her new way of being. Through the years a high steeple of strength had grown up inside her. It was time now to return to her homestead. No one saw her coming and, yet, when she slid through a crack in the wall the greeting was enormous.

FLY

Rising out of the dust
we are small particles
of clean air
coming toward you.

Already,
we've passed through
the dark side of the river.
Can't you see us?

Yesterday
we were no bigger
than bats
bumping into things.

Today
we're the perched owls
hooting in the trees.
Even in blindness
our wings can see.

FLY

Fly kept playing it safe until the day when her wings grew too large for the nest. "Off you go," said Mother Love, "for the world is big and you have much to learn."

Fly had a soft feathery body and would have preferred to stay home. Being somewhat of a stranger, she would often distance herself from the other birds who seemed to know where they were going. Fly was more like a bat than a bird.

Whenever she tried lifting her body she would bump into other flying creatures that were bigger than she was. Fly didn't have the confidence of these bigger birds and was afraid to stretch her wings for fear they would break. On a scale of one to ten, Fly would always be the last in line to take a chance.

Although Fly secretly knew that the way Mother Love had created her was good, she sometimes wished it could be different. One day when Fly stopped trying so hard a strong wind swooped down under her and propelled her forward. This time she could fly in all directions and no one could stop the momentum of her flight. Her small, frail body grew tough and strong in the wind but inside Fly there was still something missing.

Fly was really a people person but not everyone knew that. More than anything she wanted to love others but each time she tried a thick curtain of fear would wrap itself around her. She would sometimes hide for days in the narrow confines of her mind imagining what it would be like if she could be free. Anyone with a keen eye would have seen that Fly was a caged in bird who needed to navigate her own destiny in a way that would be different from others.

For the most part, the soul of Fly was something she kept concealed and, yet, it was the brightest part of her being. One day when the Call of the Mother returned, the soul of Fly popped open.

Mother Love, now Mother Wind, had always been there for her daughter but somehow a wall had grown between them. Whether it was the Mother's armour or Fly's armour it didn't really matter because whatever it was that drew them apart was now drawing them together.

At the sight of Mother Love's radiant face, Fly could hardly contain herself. "Here I am, Mother Wind," she said. "Hurl me as far as I can go and if it be your wish further still."

HUMILITY

Once
you were a timid voice
coming out
of the closet
a small speck of God
but now
you have grown
into something big.

The shape of your mouth
is as wide as the sea
and only God
can fit into it.

Hidden
in the shadow of your hand
everything appears immense
fingers
no bigger than toes
and under them
a tiny morsel of Light
so large
you can hardly see.

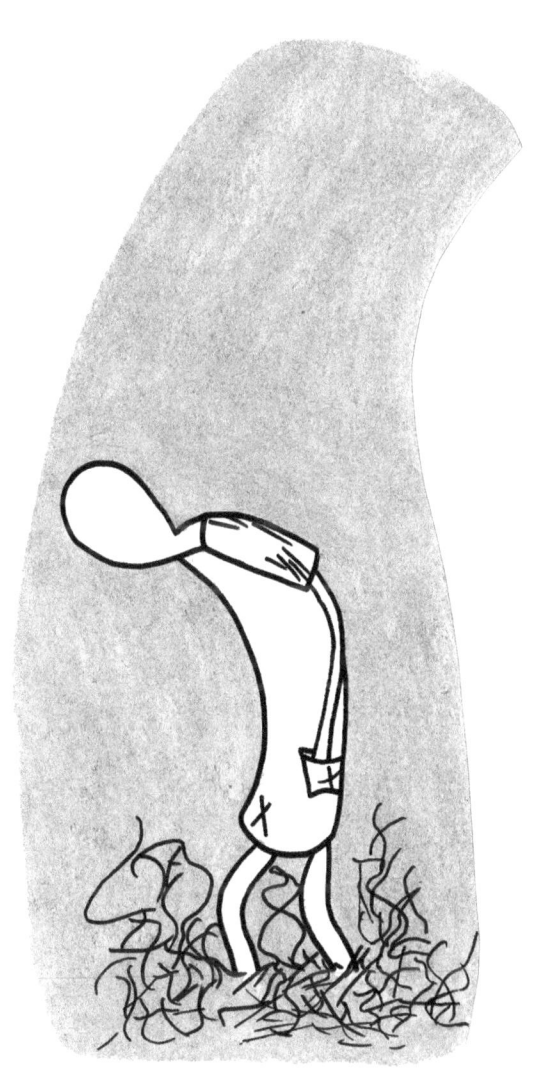

HUMILITY

Fiercely independent and strong willed like her Mother, Humility had a cushioned heart that would cause her to grow differently than other members in the family.

Right from the start, she abhorred crowds and saw them as her enemy. Introverted by nature, she would often sit on the beach, inconspicuous as an oyster in a shell. Even though she pretended to be strong, if the tide changed and a wave of adversity came toward her, she would run to the first shelter she could find.

Hiding was a game she became expert at and when no one was watching she would crouch way down low. In the public arena you don't shed tears, but here in the underground she could welcome a deluge of them.

Muttering to herself, she would sometimes say, "It's undesirable to be so sensitive," and, yet, for Humility, if a knife pierced her the wrong way, she somehow knew the imprint wouldn't remain forever.

After enough onslaughts, Humility came to believe that tragedy would create the stamina to make her whole. She never tried to defend herself. She just said, "What is, is" and left it at that.

Years later, and in all innocence, Humility put on a new garb for the world to see. She came out of hiding and strutted around like a peacock flaring her tail. Inexperienced as she was, Humility thought she knew things but ignorance soon taught her otherwise.

She definitely had gifts but none of them were developed. Wanting to expose her talents ahead of time, she was like a flashlight shining in the dark. If anything, her gifts were miniscule and you got to see only a glimmer of them.

Failing to produce her goods, the once proud Humility had no more desire to perform for anyone. With nowhere to go and no more acknowledgement from anyone, she wanted to hide herself in a blanket the size of a graveyard but people kept pushing her forward. It was not her time to die yet.

Inside, she felt like a shriveled leaf, dwindling its way down to nothing. Zero was the place of her new home and the dwelling where she would begin to rebuild herself.

Having learned her lessons well, Humility no longer dreamed of having a frill in her bonnet. She liked herself the way she was and others liked her that way, too. At last, she was an alive woman without an ounce of stuffiness in her.

Unassumingly, she would walk into a room with a knapsack on her back. Before sitting down, if there was something false in the room she would sense it immediately, the same way she sensed truth before it was spoken. She saw what she saw and no way could a façade be built around her. Daily, she sat with truth and derived nourishment from it.

PARADOX

Standing
on top of a broken bridge
you could be falling
into a chasm
and still not know
where you're going.

Up down
down up
an escalator
doesn't question
the route
the way we humans do.

We've got to go higher
up over the mountain
to the other side of day
to the place
where the dark face of God
lies hidden in the moonlight.

We need colour in our veins
turquoise blue and indigo red
we need to be children again
to paint the sky green
to live lavishly
before the day is over.

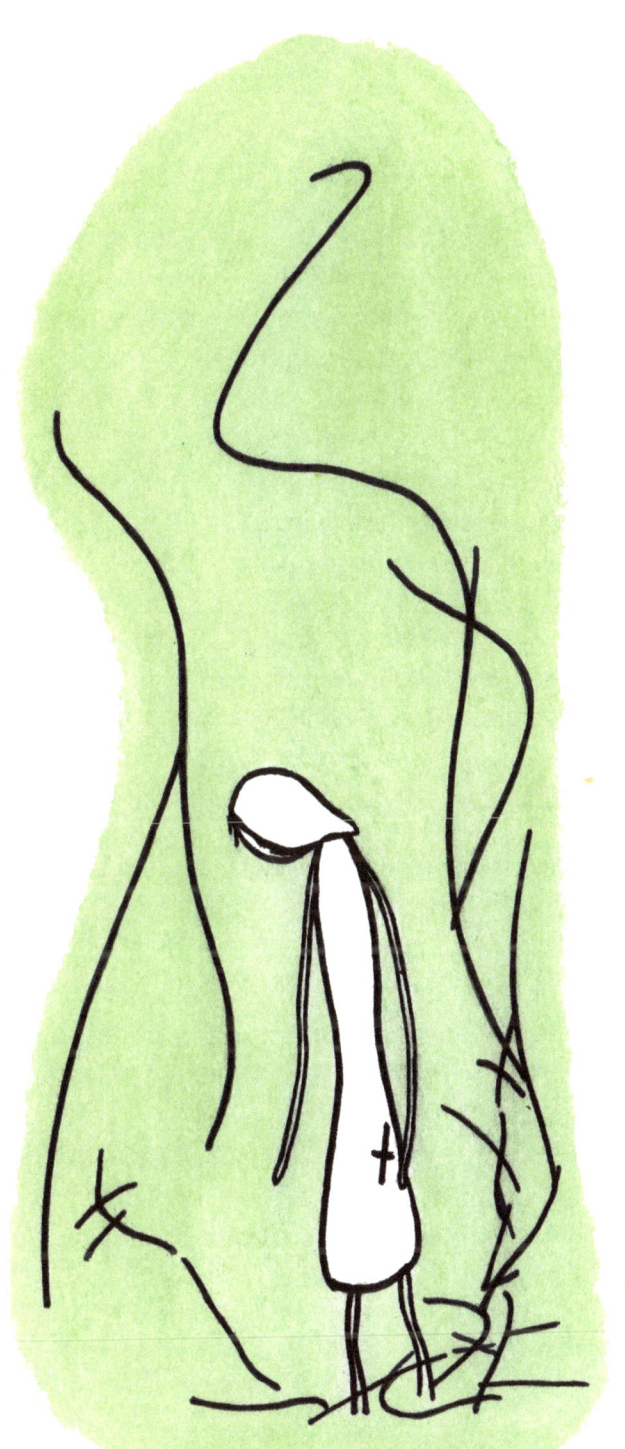

PARADOX

Paradox is a midnight wanderer. Her mind never goes to bed on time and when it does she drags the flaws of the day under the covers with her. She lives with duality and travels in those sleepless zones called insanity at bedtime. If you give her a clean sheet instead of the early morning spotted one, she'll wrestle with it as if there was something wrong with her daytime living. Give her a soft pillow and she'll tell you it's hard on the inside.

Paradox lives in a world of opposites. She hates failure and perfection is her downfall. She can't handle stains of any kind. Whether it be her own imperfections or the furniture she tarnishes, it's all one and the same. She's not at home in her home.

Paradox is like a chess player. She knows all the right moves but never wins a game. Her closest companion is frustration and after that monotony. Absurdity is a close third and drives her to worry about the smallest things. Spilling coffee on her brand new garment can upset her agenda for the entire day. And then, there's vanity. A grey streak running through the back of her hair can age her in minutes. Even if the hairdresser says it's stylish, if the world labels it ugly, you can be sure Paradox will label it uglier still.

You don't have to tell Paradox she's an extremist. She already knows it. She went to the best school of learning for her education and has the right papers to prove it. At the top of her degree you can be sure sophistication is not attached to it and if you ask her for her credentials she'll most probably tell you she has none.

Paradox is an enigma. If you give her the exact letters of the alphabet and tell her to study them well she'll tell you life isn't like that. With or without books, she's intuitive and doesn't go snooping for knowledge unless she has to. If you find her poking her head out of the left side of her brain it usually means she'll come dashing out on the right.

Being a creative thinker, you can't put Paradox in a box anymore than you can put a dog on a leash and say, "Go!" Freedom is what she prizes and just when you think you've got her cornered she'll pop up from under a closed lid and say, "Boo!"

It's not usual for people to come out of a glum room dancing for joy, but with Paradox you can expect anything. Her soul is usually one step ahead of her body and like a gymnast on a springboard each time she jumps high, she wants higher still.

You can't fool Paradox. She knows life from having lived it the way a pigeon knows home before she gets there.

HOLY REBELLION

You cannot hold on
to the hand that clutches you
anymore than you can hold on
to a hierarchical system
that would engrave your face in stone.

Knowing
how horrific strangulation is
you must cut the cord
that binds you.

Only then will you know
it takes more than a chisel
or torrent of turbulent air
to propel a person forward.

Breaking free of rigidity,
the work of a rebel
is not to pollute the air
but to make it clean.

It's a call
to start paving the way
for a road
that's never been built.

How you get there
will be determined not by gravity
but by a Force that will wield you
where you have never gone before.

HOLY REBELLION

Rebellion was not born rebellious. In fact, there was not a bone in her body that would have crushed anyone. Born into a family that loved her, the timid Rebellion was a quiet, sensitive girl.

Before stepping out into the big world, nothing threatened her. She could soar like a bird in her own skin and feel at home anywhere. As for loving God, no one needed to teach her anything. She came into the world knowing how to do it. God's love was the spa she secretly bathed in.

Early in life, and unbeknown to others, Rebellion was already developing peculiar habits. If you approached her with harsh words or a disapproving look, she would instantly turn into a nobody. Rather than speak, she would become the invisible shy girl, whose lips closed inward with the word silent imprinted on her tongue.

At school, Rebellion was an anomaly. She disliked stupidity but somehow that was the desk she sat in. Shut down, locked in, question and answer period would leave her mind in a freeze. Each time she wanted to speak, something would grip her. It might have been ignorance or terror. Whatever it was it felt like a padlock had been placed over her mouth. Other children around her seemed to be thriving and why she couldn't was beyond her.

One day she felt a surge of hope. It was the day

after she left the world of academia and embarked on a new path, the path she had always felt at home in. Rebellion, you see, was spiritual, deeply spiritual. This was her territory and she knew she could thrive in it. What she didn't know was that God's stairway had crooked steps, not the little girl steps she had been used to and that it would take a lifetime to climb them.

Rebellion was older now and God's voice was sterner. Each time Rebellion wanted to go up, the Voice would say, "Down!" Having a strict, loving friend as her teacher, Rebellion often felt like a puppy in training. Whoever this God was, he/she, Rebellion always felt she could trust the One who created her, even when the trusting hurt.

One day God said, "Rebellion, I am going to give you a mirror and I want you to look into it." Reluctantly, Rebellion summoned up her courage and when she looked inside the window of her soul, this is what she saw. Chaos and herself in it, kicking down the walls of her being and destroying the establishment in which she lived.

This time, God the Mother, chided her and said: "Not any amount of kicking can establish you in peace. Only love can do this and not until you have learned to love will the walls come down that you are trying to kick."

Rebellion was a slow learner but she did learn. Through many long years, her deafened ears adjusted to the clear, clean sound of the Mother, and it was her music she chose to follow.

ECSTASY

One day soul child was seen
carrying a trinity of birds
in her knapsack.

The music was unseen, unheard
but definitely ethereal
and known only to the listener.

From then on
whenever soul child
entered a house
the Energy in the room
became different.

Out of her feet
she could sprout wings
that made her fly.

In a body
physically close to you
she could be wave lengths away
and still remain intimate
as a cloud hugging you
after its spill of rain.

ECSTASY

Right from the start, Ecstasy was different. She disliked the humdrum world of human beings she had been born into. When people weren't watching, she would shrink into something small, a lizard, a frog, a toad, anything to make herself invisible. A tiny creature at best, her thin skin tore easily and she knew the colour of blood before it manifested. Early in life, she learned that death, like fear, was the skeleton she carried with her.

Coping with life, was not one of her best skills, and yet, she had a survival kit that made it easier. She named the kit, "God in my rocker," and would go there whenever melancholy set in. In her rocker, she could woo herself into a lullaby that chased away any former feeling of despair. Ecstasy often wondered if God lived in the rocker or was it that God lived in her? Either way, the rocker brought her untold comfort, peace and tranquility.

Ecstasy had highly developed senses. She could see dirt, smell dirt, taste dirt, swallow dirt, and even though it didn't make her ill, one day it would. Surprisingly enough, it would be the dirt, the very enemy that had tried to destroy her, that would make her well again. Coughing it all up, was not an easy task, but a long, laborious one she would have liked to avoid.

Eventually, Ecstasy applauded herself for making the journey home. Returning to her roots, she grew red wings that could breathe fire into you. From then on her growth was phenomenal and no one could stop it.

Living beyond the sun, the moon and the stars, she let her aspirations carry her as far as they would go. Hers was a radiance beyond radiances, that could no longer get trampled over by the boots that people wore.

For the return trip, Ecstasy put on a new set of clothes, the kind that people wear. Mistaken by some to be a mysterious astronaut or unseen visitor from another planet, Ecstasy soon made herself at home.

No longer estranged, she came into the world knowing who she was. Nothing had changed but she had changed. Her eyes were large, bright and beautiful. This time nothing disturbed her, not even the sharp edged rocks that came tumbling down the cliff to greet her.

It seemed that everyone was her friend, and if there were enemies, which there were, she grew to loving them. Enemies, she said, carried the trademark of a teacher and what you didn't know you could learn from them.

For Ecstasy, everything had a purpose. Even dirt glowed in the dark and was like nectar to her tongue. In the same way, disfigured faces or distortions of any kind, carried the holy in them and were to be treated with reverence and respect. All of life was precious and no one was exempt from loving the dark, the dirty and the ugly. All was part of God's beautiful plan and Ecstasy was at home in it.

MELANCHOLY JOY

When you know
devastation
is an empty plate
hungry enough
to devour you
will you flee from her
or will you say:

"Here comes God
stomping the sadness
out of me!"

Yes, dear melancholy,
it's time to admit
that a face caved in on itself
is not where you want to be.

That's why God's tongue
is longer than yours
and fits into your mouth
sideways.

It's the adrenalin
of Someone loving you!

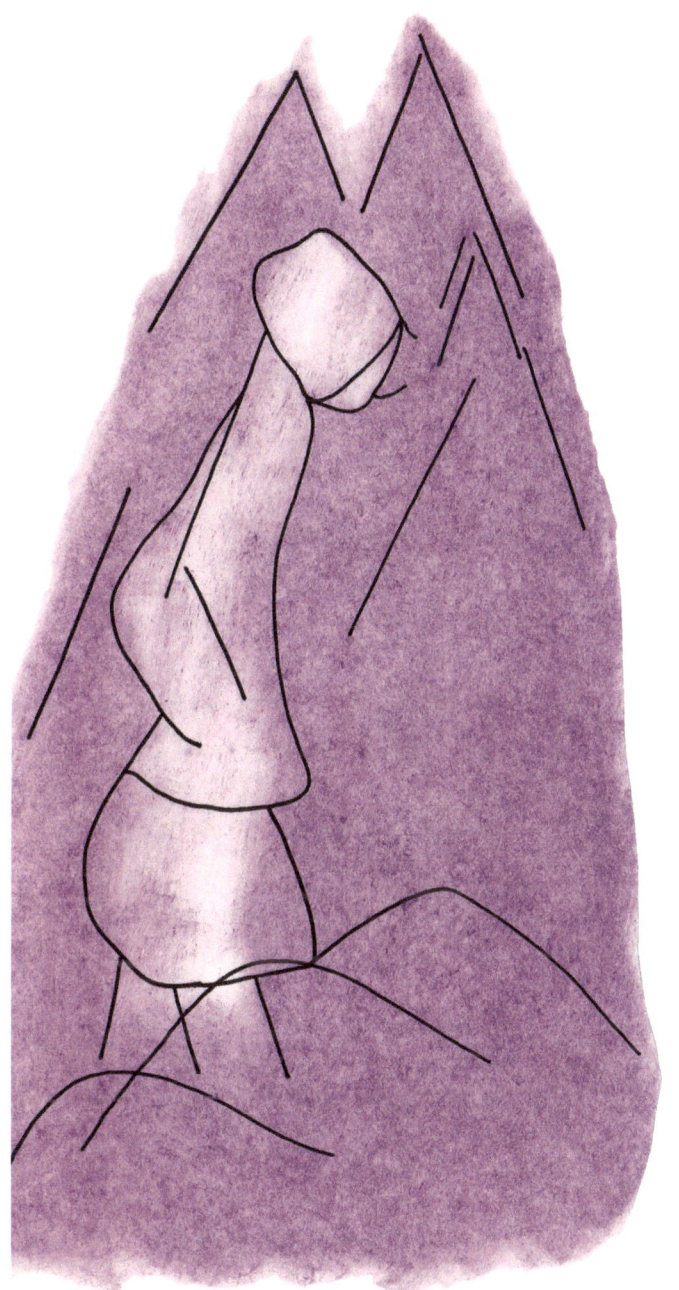

MELANCHOLY JOY

Melancholy Joy had a personality that would have befuddled anyone. She was like a chameleon, moody on the inside but joyful on the out. With closed eyes, she could see things in the dark, bats flying, objects moving. Everything was big and she was small.

In a world that frightened her, Melancholy Joy was a lost soul that found God in the strangest of places. Feeling dismal, she could whistle a tune out of nowhere and God would come on the ripple of a wind, unseen, unheard, but she knew he was there.

Being somewhat of a misfit, Melancholy Joy despised labeling people. She said there was something treacherous in it. Even her own name had a cobweb dangling from it. "Melancholy," she said, "implies something negative, something lesser than who I am."

Not everyone understood Melancholy Joy. In fact, few did. With little to say, she would enter a room, pretending to be there and, yet, if ever there was a stranger in a crowd you could count on Melancholy Joy to be first in line.

Early in life, she concealed her identity, a strange habit she could never quite erase. Like a whirlwind in the trees, she could be feeling dizzy and, yet, appear placid in the middle of a storm. When things worsened and hardship covered her, she would go on singing God's name but soon even that lost its lustre. Falling into a lifeless pit, she finally admitted that it was her poison and not someone else's resting in the dung of her heart.

With this kind of devastation, nothing could shake Melancholy Joy out of her lethargy, until the day when she felt the blast of a machine gun; a blast of sadness flattening her as she had never been flattened before. God was nowhere to be found and, yet, picking herself up she found the real face she had been looking for. At last, she knew the game of hiding was over.

This time Love grew roots in the basement of her being, roots bigger than she could have imagined. Green roots, yellow roots, purple roots. There was no end to the vast range of colour coming into her. It was Infinity at its best and she knew it.

She had entered a new era of sunrise. Standing on the horizon, she could see a Light coming toward her, a Light that would no longer mean closing doors or running into dark cupboards for safety.

It was a day of celebration, a great day where Mother earth and all the creatures in it rejoiced with her. It was a coming home day where people got invited to the party. No longer was she a stranger to herself or anyone.

Having remained concealed for so long, it was like having a veil lifted. For the first time, Melancholy Joy loved her name and others loved it too. Even at night she could hear her name being sung. It was a good name and she had struggled hard to get it.

GIRL CHILD SINGS

Beside the stumbling feet
of a small child
loneliness
built her nest
inside a tree.

Circuiting around the child
she said:
"Without branches
I am the naked one
of this stripped down tree
and you the fogged in one
who cannot see.

Know this,
my destined daughter,
I will grow you up
and shatter you down.
Only then
when the sky turns red
will you know
I bleed when you bleed.

How else
can the bark
of a pierced-open tree
sing?"

GIRL CHILD SINGS

Without voice, Girl Child could have been a leaf stammering in the wind, but she was more than that, much more. On the outside, she may have appeared fragile as the cracked up shell of an egg but on the inside she housed the feisty spirit of a dragon that carried enough heat to sustain her through the winter days.

In spite of her timidity, Girl Child had an uncanny way of knowing things. Wired differently than others, she could sense danger from a distance. It was the enemy she dreaded most, the monster a child sees in the movies and runs from. Wanting to lock the door on the monster, but not knowing how to defend herself, Girl Child let danger come in. Sometimes all it took was a slap on the hand, a harsh look or an angry word, to crush that which was soft within her.

For Girl Child, danger could mean almost anything but the feel of it was always the same, a thick edged sword going through her. Even in adulthood, she allowed herself to be pushed outside the crowd until she would disappear over the black horizon of her smaller self.

Through the years, Girl Child had painstakingly built walls to protect herself, walls that would one day become obsolete, torn down and left in ruin. As distasteful as this was, it would plunge Girl Child into an adult woman who would spin her web differently.

Living outside the parameters of sophistication, she would often be seen driving a vehicle that was bigger than she was. Even though she was a purposeful driver, wanting a direct route to Infinity, she would often be seen losing her way.

Estranged from herself and the world in which she lived, all that Girl Child had ever wanted to do was to sing the Song of her soul. It was a Song unlike any other and she had come into the world singing it.

Finally, on a war torn beach in winter, she opened her mouth full of Song to the sea. Whether others understood it or not, no longer mattered. This time she heard it as if for the first time:

"Child, in your un-guardedness, you have taught me what others never have been able to teach me, that my look should be as open as yours, and that my eyes should know Beauty from having perceived it in you."

MOUNTAIN CLIMBER

A small kernel of life
bursting out of her shell
the exuberant one
arrived at the summit
of a mountain
before she had climbed it.

Rushing to the finish line
any climber
could have told her:
a mountain
hanging on the edge
of a cliff
is doomed to die
but she did not listen.

Lured on by Love
even a crushed foot
could not have stopped her
from entering the womb
a second time.

Giving birth to a Son
who would unchain the world
she would be a forerunner
of all women
who would do the same.

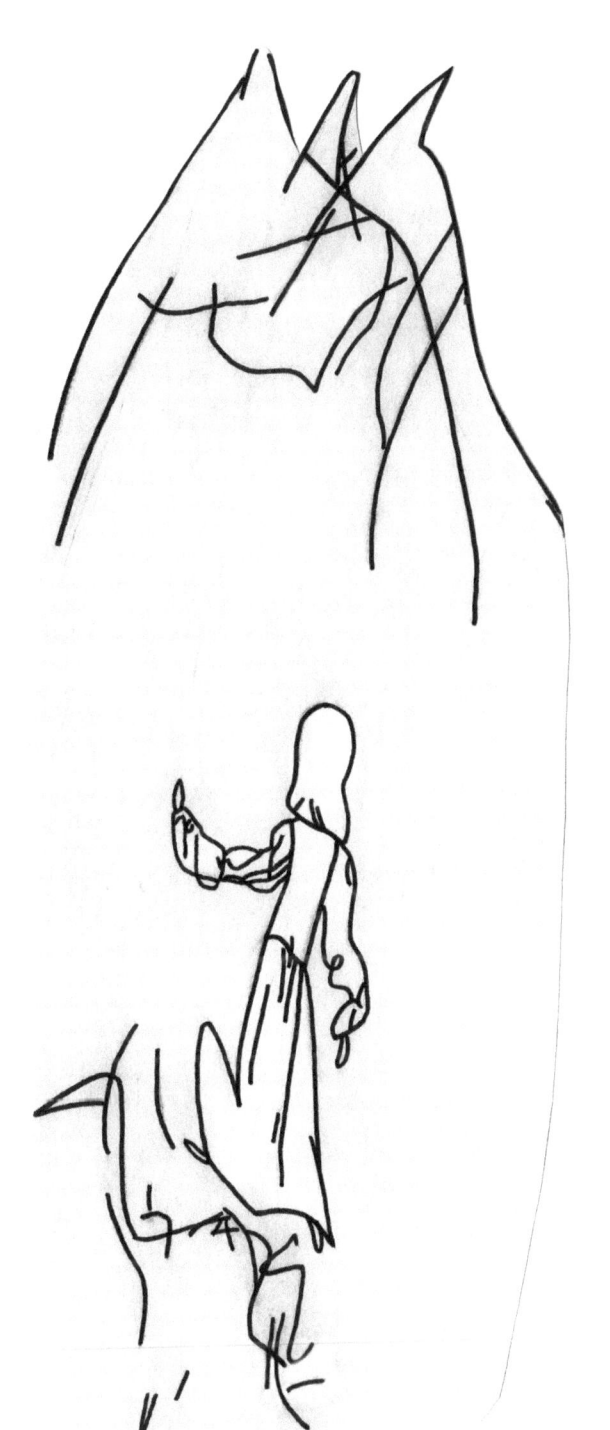

MOUNTAIN CLIMBER

Forging a new path, Mountain Climber sat still. "Today," she said, "the plucking will begin." With her prickly fingers, she began whisking the weeds out of her soul. "How did you get into my home," she said, "when I didn't know you were there?"

Sneakily, the black, ugly beasts replied: "We are the naughty bugs living inside your caged in self. Each time you go about doing good, no one applauds you and we remind you of that. When you want to succeed, we tell you how badly you've failed and you believe us."

"Yes," she said, "I know all that. You are my other self, the critical one whose eyes slant inward. Seeking approval, you mirror my own hunger and I will no longer be the garbage can for the disposal of your goods. If you must kill me, do it now, for I can no longer be prey to your insidious ways."

Ripping away the old self, Mountain Climber plunged forward into a terrain that would both flatten and free her. Becoming her real self, meant that the idyllic mask had to go. She often wondered about masks, whether other people wore them or was it just her silly self wanting to appear different.

Always wanting to succeed, Mountain Climber soon learned that rushing up a mountain had a down side to it. Tumbling backwards, no one could stop her from moving forward, not even Mountain Climber herself.

Having seen the face of God once, and urged on by it, she hurriedly travelled to the summit but no one was there. Just a grey streak running through the face of a stone, reminding her that you cannot cling to the glitter, once it is gone.

Swallowing her pride, Mountain Climber returned to the land of her birth. No longer looking for approval, the pivotal ground on which she stood, welcomed her. Already she could feel the hard walls cracking and with it the old self unraveling.

It was a slow, tedious journey, and not without knowledge, that she watched the barriers that had locked her in come down. Even disenchantment, betrayal and anger, came in through the door to heal her. Everyone and everything was welcome. It was the unmistakable new face of God she had been looking for!

COCOON BREAKER

Asleep in my cocoon
she's the hand
inside my body
the anonymous One
whose name I know.
Love has a face
and it's hers.

Loosening my taut nerves
she spreads a soft blanket
over me
and to my hardened cells
she says,
"Live!"

I cannot open fast enough
and, yet,
she tells me
there's a tunnel to go through.

Quieting
the fierce noise within me
she places her smooth mouth
over mine
and with the Voice of her melody
I sing and I sing and I sing!

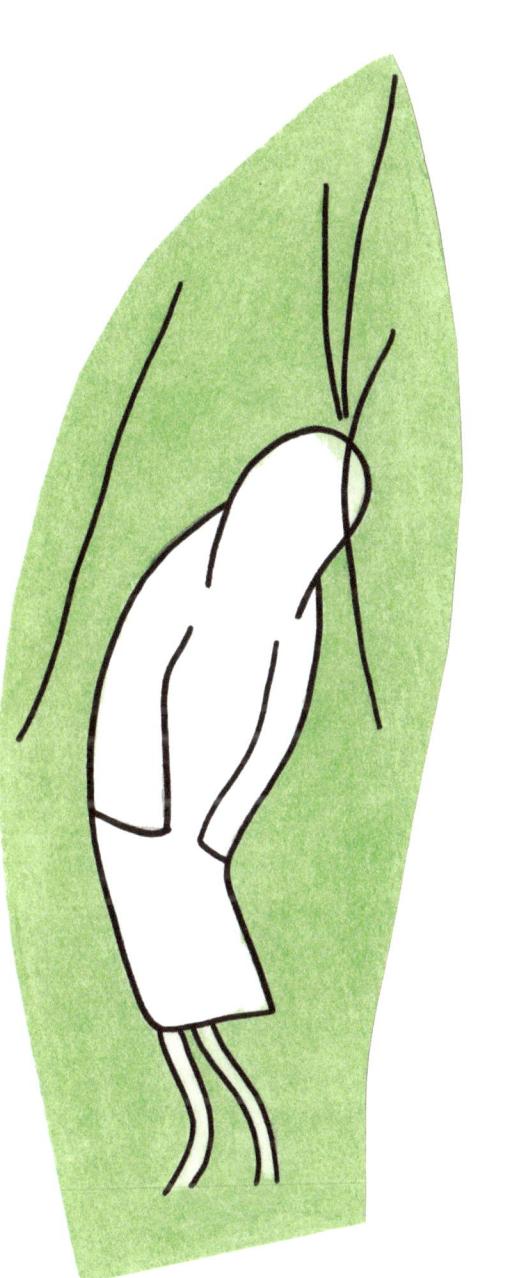

COCOON BREAKER

Cocoon Breaker lived in an underground world with tough skin hardened all around her. Early in life, she started distancing herself from others, putting up barriers and fence posts, that kept people out of her territory. She was a type of architect who built her home on unsteady ground.

Barring people out, no one really knew where or how she lived. Everything was kept secret. When people asked her about her body, she would say, "What's that, the vehicle that gets me around by bumping into things?" She was both fascinated and terrified by this vehicle that often had no sense of direction.

Another scary place was bedtime. That's when the monsters came out. Nobody had told her that emotions live in the body and are strangers that can play havoc with you. Not knowing who she was she would say, "Who am I?" and, of course, there never was an answer.

Even if she had heard Jesus say, "I am who I am," she would have been too young to understand. Eventually, she would acquire that kind of knowledge but not until she had gone through the hoops that would bring her to maturity.

In her growing up years, Cocoon Breaker played the game of pretend. Appearance became important to her and even her wardrobe suggested a kind of sophistication that was far from being genuine.

As much as she pretended to be intelligent, if someone placed her in a box with a closed lid, that would be the best indicator of how much she really knew. Being confined in this way, she lived inside herself with a teetering wall that could have collapsed had anyone pushed it.

Finally, after years of drudgery and in a moment of despair, "I Am who I Am," became Cocoon Breaker's best friend. This time she knew the Jesus journey and the venture was on.

Thrust forward by the wind of a ferocious Spirit, she let herself be carried in a caravan to places she had never been before. She named her new journey, "God of the unknown way."

It was a time of breakthrough, a knowing time that heralded in the best and worst of life's journey. Free at last, Cocoon Breaker let the Light come in and to the holy One she said: "Keep singing your Song within me. It's a good one and I will sing it forever."

OCEAN SURVIVOR

Destined
for the higher seas
I was told
a small boat
travelling off course
will get you nowhere.

So, here I am
sitting on the edge
of a sinking ship
going down
into the basement
of the sea.

In this rudderless zone
you don't navigate
the ocean
it navigates you.

Losing control
even the waves stammer
become speechless
in your Presence.

If you are a loving God
and I know you are
I wish I could say
this is a dream I awaken from
unscathed, whole and complete
but I cannot.

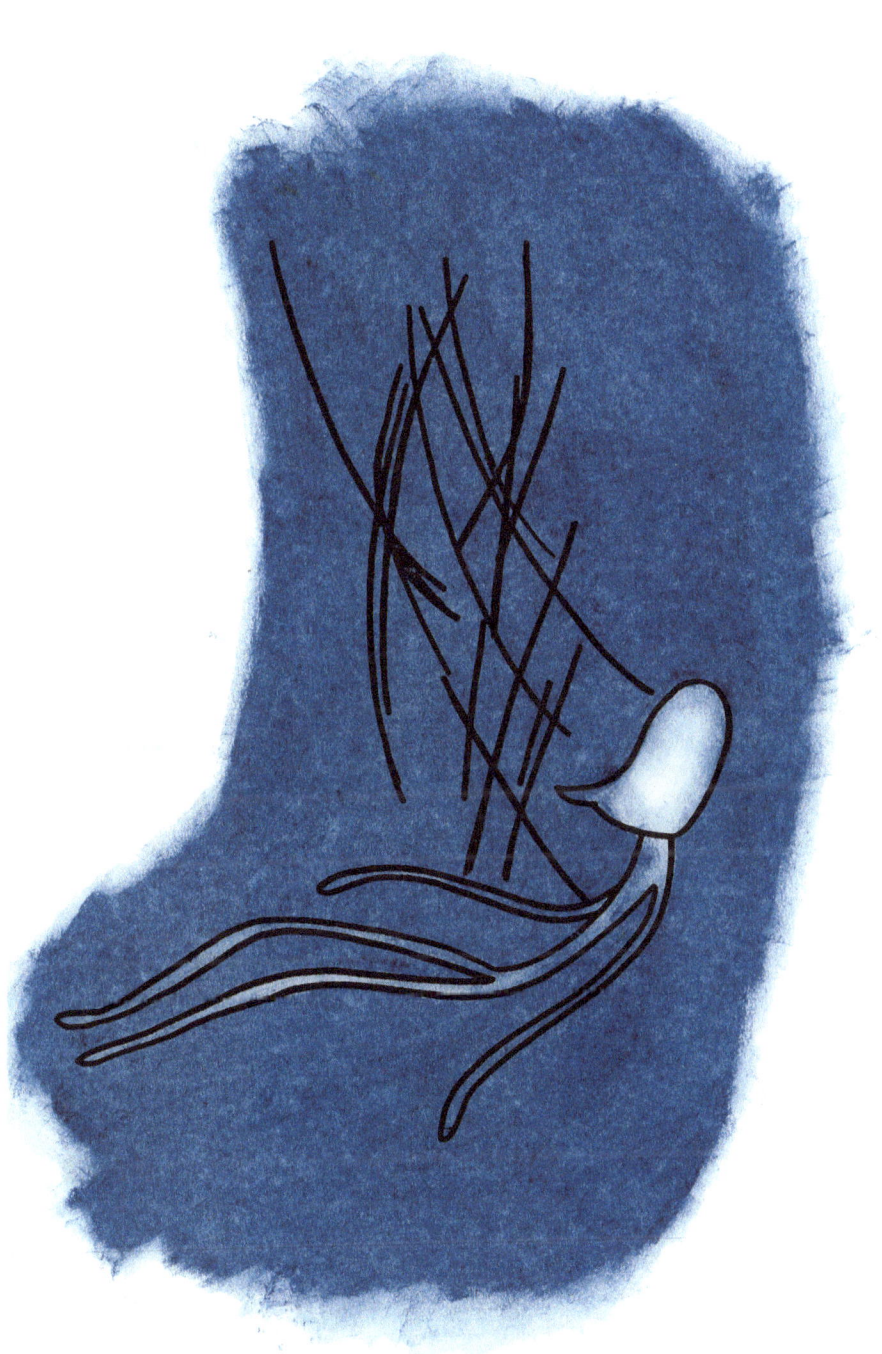

OCEAN SURVIVOR

Ocean Survivor had an insatiable thirst for God. Perhaps it was a love affair that began in the beginning, when God created the heavens and the earth and placed her in the farthest corner of the sea.

With a voracious appetite and always wanting to be first, Ocean Survivor was a small fish who never could be satisfied. Her life was always about more, more, more. Drinking up the last dregs of the water, she could be having a full meal and still be wanting another morsel. Soon enough, God became aware of her tactics and knew that something needed to be done about her gluttonous nature.

When the fish came swarming in, Ocean Survivor would try sitting in a preferential position but she never got to see God that way. God would disappear on her and she would call out, "Where are you?" and then the love affair would begin again. Feeling small, she soon learned that an empty bucket in the sea could only be filled by the One who loved her.

As she grew older, God would leave her more often, sometimes lying in a coffin, desolate on the bottom of the sea. If anything made Ocean Survivor belligerent, it was the trickster part of God saying that abandonment was good for her.

Being somewhat of a rebellious nature, Ocean Survivor often wrestled with God. What irked her most was why she had to be the smallest of the small fish when she wanted to be the biggest of the big fish. Learning to be herself was not an easy task. Sometimes she wondered if God had stymied her into a corner so that one day she would survive the trauma of the sea.

Years later when Ocean Survivor was getting old and scraggly, she pushed God into the turbulent waters. Surprised by her own strength and discovering how playful God could be, the love affair took on a wilder dimension. God could be big and God could be small and pretty soon she thought, God could be anything!

With water gurgling through her nostrils, Ocean Survivor let God take her on the journey of a lifetime. Coaxing her up onto the land, God said, "Take my hand and together we will explore the vastness of your becoming." Already she could feel the rush of Infinity going through her. Instantly mesmerized by the sweep and intensity of it, she knew there would be no turning back.

SUNRISE

Stop tiptoeing
around the closed door
of this locked room.
It's the silhouette
of your old self
telling you not to go there.

Chopping off
the rungs of a ladder
you need to climb higher
to where the wheel
of your smaller self
spins you upward.

In this holy air
you can be yourself
your soul
can be the matchbox
that sets your heart
on fire.

No longer stuck
in the wax
of a candle
you can glow now.

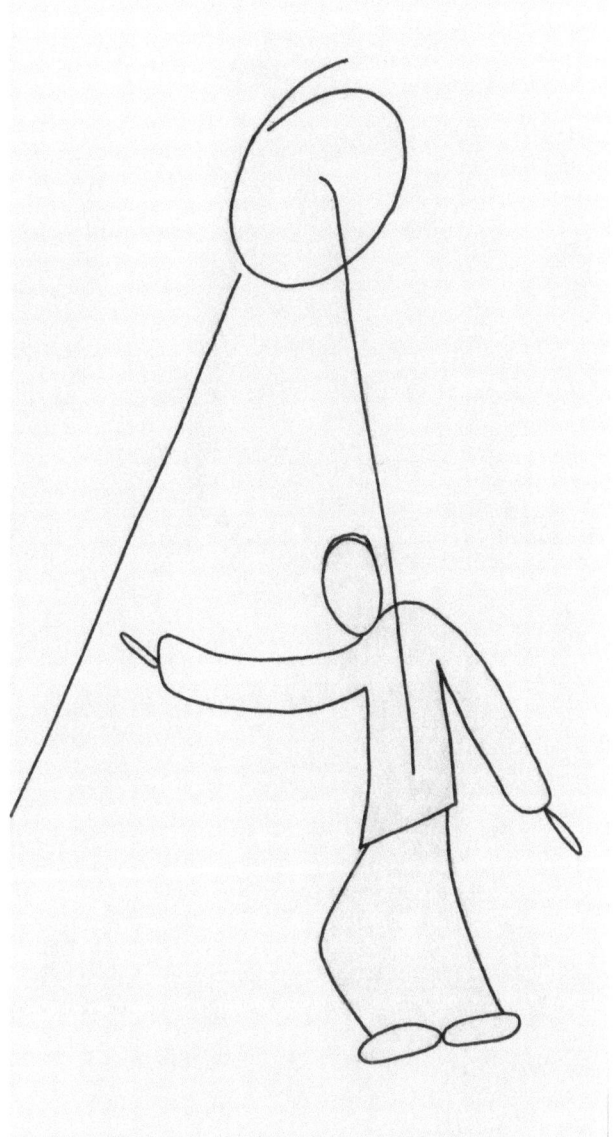

SUNRISE

Sunrise, as people knew her, was not a stuffy person. She presented herself well and won the admiration of many. What people didn't see was the façade behind the façade. On the outside, Sunrise was no different than others but on the inside the crowing of a rooster could be heard. It was the early morning signal that would hoist her out of bed.

Before going anywhere, Sunrise would cup her small hands around her ears, listening for the keener sound of the day. It was a hush that was already there before she was there and she named it, "God of all being."

Before starting her day, the workaholic Sunrise would let God into her room and then close the door shut. The shut door was for keeping others out but somehow she knew God would always find a way in. Her room was messy and even though God didn't mind the clutter, she did.

One day before going to work, she admitted to God that she didn't like rote prayers. In a nonchalant way God replied, "I've known that for a long time. It's pretty obvious that the messy scraps lying on the floor of your supposedly well-ordered room belong to you." "Yes," she replied, and went off to work in a huff.

Once the busyness of the day was upon her, Sunrise somehow got zippered into it and forgot God's early morning sarcastic remark.

Even in the midst of work, Sunrise loved being quiet and often thought that this was her form of prayer. Not being born loquacious, she often found herself in a quandary. When the world was full of noise, she was silent. On occasions like this, the air around her and the people in it would seem to bristle, waiting for a word to be spoken when there was none.

If Sunrise had a doorway into her soul, which she did, anyone could have seen her Light from a distance but the time had not come for such an exposure and she knew it. "Wisdom," she said, "sits in a vacuum for years before the words get spoken." Sunrise knew this in the same way she knew green buds are bitter, a holocaust to be endured before they ripen.

With this kind of knowledge, the window of God became wide enough for the whole world to see. On the day of her second birth, Sunrise climbed through the window with God in the lead.

FRAGILITY

When my petals open
you will see me
as I am
not as you
envisioned me to be.

Being dragged through
a field of daisies
I could have told you
I would rot there
but you did not listen.

Turmoil
has been my teacher
has ripped me open
to tell you
a small girl
inside the shaking body
of a woman
lives here.

Hard as an acorn
fragility
has cracked me open
touch my petals
and you will see.

FRAGILITY

Fragility was born into a world that had hard spikes in it. Being a naive journeyer, she started out on the road of life loving others and presuming that others would love her in return. She soon learned that a soft nature like hers was an irritant to some and a blessing to others.

The tools in Fragility's kit were not equipped to deal with harshness and, so, where did it go? Underground, into a bin called nasty. What Fragility didn't know was that repressed feelings are like slivers under the skin. They produce their own kind of poison and whether the person is aware of it or not an energy of falsity gets emitted.

As much as Fragility wanted to change her personality, she couldn't. She just wasn't born to be mean and, yet, one day she would have to contend with the dark forces that were in her too.

What she needed to learn was that the plan of God was for everyone to live together, the good and the bad, the ugly and the beautiful. It was the alchemy of God that would polish up the world and make it shine. As much as she wanted the gold of that promise, she didn't like the alchemy to get there.

Trudging into her own darkness was a painful passage. Sweet became bitter. Sour became tart. Sometimes she would chew on this unpleasant food for days and sometimes years at a time. When the food became increasingly rancid, too rancid to taste, it was the moment of her awakening.

What Fragility needed most was to love herself. Others could have told her this but only when she knew it for herself could the armour come down that she had been trying to wear. It was a slow, tedious journey, where layer by layer she began peeling off the dust of the years.

Finally, the victory was hers. It was her hour of alchemy and everyone knew it when she stood up and said:

"Stand high in Love. Do not stifle or protect it. Let it overflow freely into the lands of your people. Let, too, the echo of your rejoicing resound in every yard, remembering to leave on the sills of those you love a blossom of your freshness. Give, give to the end, everything you have and are. Refuse your love to no one. It is the one gift you are best at."

BELOVED MESSENGER

We may have skin
the colour of rainbows
but in our off season
we shut down
we of the brown,
the drab, the grey.

Falling into an abyss
of our own making
we the desolate ones
get chewed up by it.

Losing sight
of our homeland
we see the dark-faced One
coming toward us.

Even before her arrival
we know her Voice
will be the greening of us.

Picking a thousand daisies
we'd go anywhere
to follow her.

BELOVED MESSENGER

Beloved Messenger came into the room wearing a mauve toque and purple shawl. Somewhat shabbily dressed for an elitist party, the crowd snickered and whispered amongst themselves, "How did she get in? Where are her manners or does she have any?"

Beloved Messenger knew what they were thinking and this gave her all the more reason to stay. Putting people into lesser categories was no different than pulling the stuffing out of a teddy bear.

Sitting at the back of the room as an observer, she could have been a modern day Jesus figure, man, woman, child. The gender didn't matter but who she was did matter. Anyone, including herself, didn't deserve the disrespect she was receiving.

One of the elitist group, named Judas, came late to the party. He wore the finest of jewels so others could see. Pushing himself toward centre stage, everyone applauded. None of the clothes worn that night could match his freshly painted tattoos. The colours were exquisite and well-placed all over his sagging body.

The crowd had blown up Judas into a balloon for all to see but on the inside was a man that was hurting. The more the crowd applauded, the deeper became the incision of his wound.

Beloved Messenger was no longer a silent observer. She stood up in fury, compassionately gazing at the man who no longer knew who he was or where he had come from.

If the Beloved abhorred anything it was falsity and everyone in the room knew it. Her love was fierce, fierce enough to silence the sham of the evening. It wasn't just Judas who had lost his way but the crowd that mingled with him.

Catching a glimpse of the Beloved's face, the crowd quickly reversed positions. Like dumb sheep in a pasture, they were now standing at the back of the room. No one said anything.

As people left the room, a small streak of light remained sitting upright in the chairs of those who had gathered. The people left quietly and humbly, acknowledging that Love came in as a chisel that night, to slit open what needed to be shaved away.

SERENITY

Beware
of the calm centre
of a cyclone,
it grows in you
like the blindness
of a blunt pin.

Hovering around
it's more
than the sweet tooth
of death
biting into you.

It's yourself disguised
in the white face
of a giant lamb,
the she wolf
ready to devour you.

Welcome her
as your friend.
She's the only storm
that can shake
the lethargy out of you.

Standing beside you
she's the unseen One
the torch
on the hill
lighting your way home.

SERENITY

Serenity was an old soul that came into the world carrying a heavy load. As much as she wanted to fit into society, her bent shoulders often left her on the outskirts of it. Sometimes she would ask herself: "Is it the debilitating baggage of parental ancestry that is holding me back or am I one of those lost souls carrying within me the gene of anonymity?"

Groping for the light, Serenity was never quite sure of anything other than the small bronze compass she kept hidden in her pocket. On dreary days, when darkness invaded her, she would hold the compass in her hands and sometimes God would appear with a tiny morsel of food.

As Serenity grew older, God wanted to lavish her more abundantly. She was in her seventies now and was excited to think that God would hold a party for her and that she could receive even more gifts than she had been accustomed to.

What Serenity didn't know was that God had a furnace and she would be plunged into it, fired up so that the brilliance she had been born with would shine. After the firing, God's parting words were: "Go now into the milieu I have prepared for you."

Once Serenity was transported to her new location, she found herself sitting in a crowded room. It was her turn to speak. Would she or would she not was the question? It was a ripple thought that travelled through the room. Most people knew that Serenity carried her history with her and that to break through the shell of it would be difficult.

In the past, Serenity had chosen to sit in a chair that was silent but this time she could no longer endure the pain of it. Without a flicker of embarrassment, she stood up and said: "That person gliding through the room isn't really me. It's my pseudo nature trying to make myself real."

Already the crowd was growing anxious but this time you couldn't put a muzzle on her. Serenity's words flowed like ink in a pen and she spoke with an authority that was calm and deliberate. "Superficiality", she said, "is something I gag on and, yet, it was I who chose to wear those shoes even when they didn't fit."

"I am part of the global matchstick," she said. "The dross has been burnt out of me and the lethargy is no more. From now on, I want only illumination!"

DAYBREAK

First ray of dawn
pressing in on me
that's who God is,
the hinge
behind the shut door
of my heart
prying me open.

Withered love
makes me thirsty
downcast in the rain
but you,
God of the morning,
are not like that.

Dried up
you give me clean air
and a basin to wash in.

It doesn't matter
what road I take
even a detour
is travelling toward You.

Sitting
in a basket of thistles
or standing
on the horizon of a hill
nothing
will change
the way I love You.

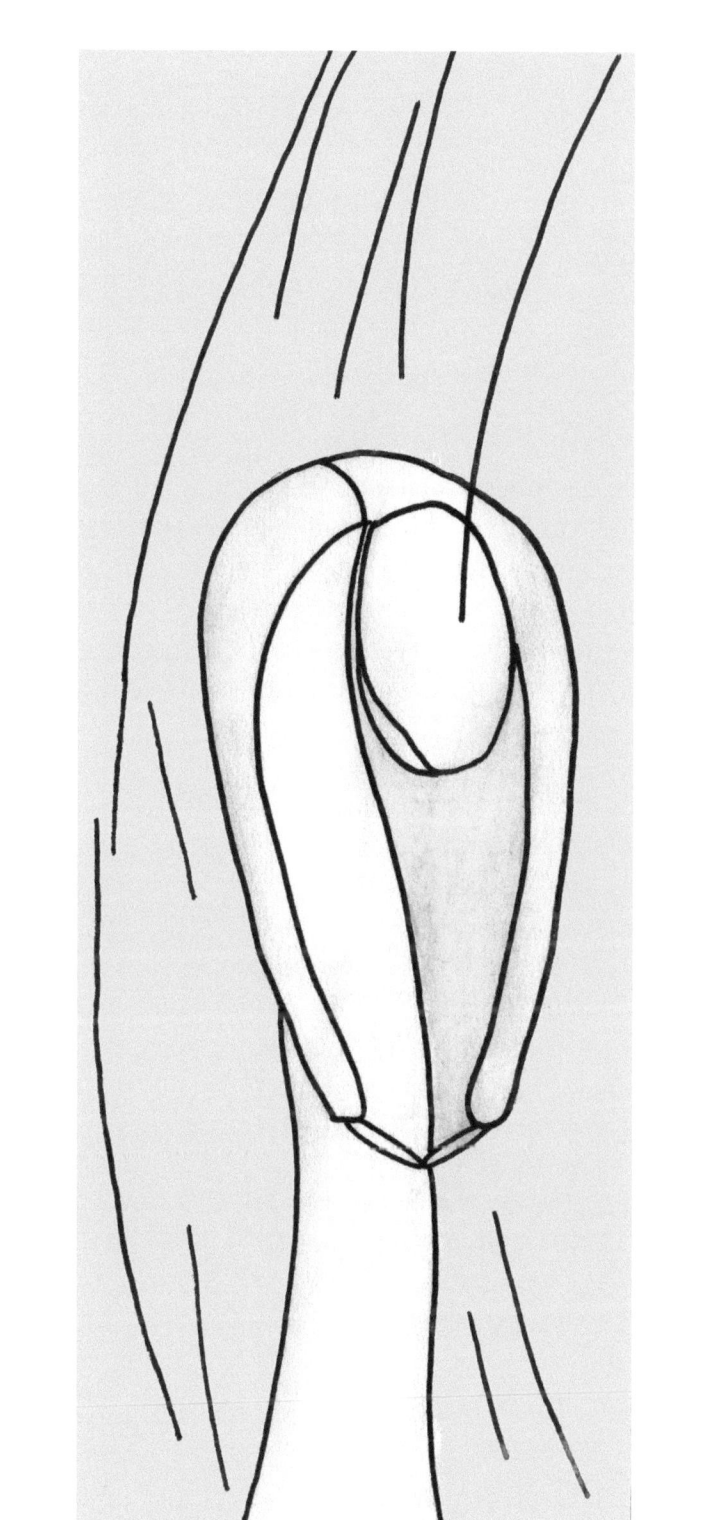

DAYBREAK

Daybreak lived in a land of light and even though there was a dark side to her nature she kept it concealed. It was the unsung part of her day that would reveal its dark, gloomy head at night.

Any meanness or unkindness of the day that had been inflicted on her would come back to haunt her in the night. It was like having the nasty buzz of a hornet rise up in the deepest crevice of her being. Even with the covers over her the hornet always had a way of getting into her bed at night which never made sleeping easy.

One night on retiring early, she fell into a deep, peaceful sleep only to be awakened by a bizarre dream. The hornet was back, buzzing around her pillow. "Get up!" the hornet said. "Clean out your ears and go look at your face in the mirror." "I can't!" said Daybreak. "You must!" said hornet. When Daybreak did as she was told what she saw was the flash of a clean face turned rusty.

On the outside, Daybreak appeared naive and innocent, but on the inside the veil was slowly being lifted. With keen eyes, keener than most, she soon discovered that the hornet was God chasing her and from that reality she knew she could no longer hide.

The next day, God found Daybreak choking on a piece of bread soaked in honey. God looked at her sternly and said, "Haven't you learned to stop sticking your tongue into the honey pot? That's for bees only. You look for love in all the wrong places and often get stung because of it."

Somewhat startled by God's comments, Daybreak still felt that of all teachers God was the best.

One day God approached her with a greater sensitivity than usual and said, "Daybreak, you're being exclusive. All people are made in my image, even the person you love who turns against you with a dagger. It's the only way the sweet, innocent, caring side of yourself can be broken open." "Oh," said Daybreak, with the tone of an ouch in it.

As hard as it was to digest the Teacher's message, Daybreak summoned all the strength she had and was receptive to it.

From then on, Daybreak began to see God in all things. The other side of night became day and wherever Daybreak went she saw life with luminosity in it.

SPIDER WOMAN

In the circus of life
not every motion
will be good for you
so centre yourself
spider girl
and be strong
for the spinning.

Soaring too high, too fast
can be just as dangerous
as sitting in a stagnant pool
of passivity
when you should be
moving forward.

Sometimes
your best learning
will come in winter
when you
like the tragic whisper
in the mouth of a snowbird
have nothing to say.

In the end
if you can paint
on the canvas of your life
what it is to be whole
you will have achieved
what you came for.

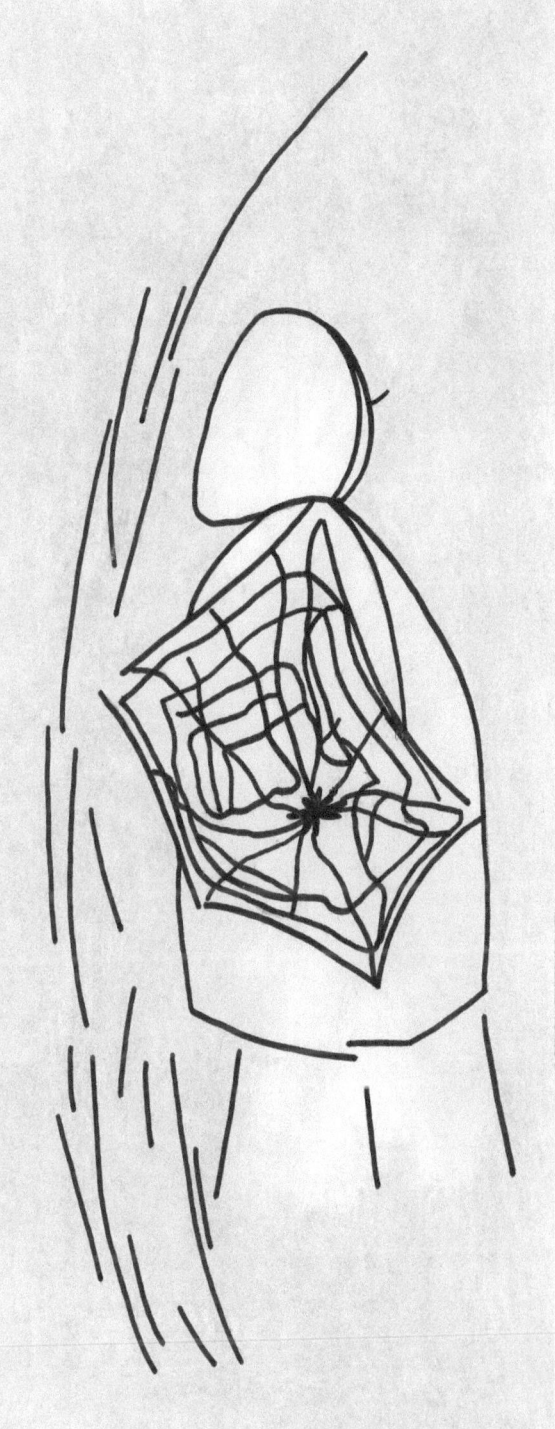

SPIDER WOMAN

Spider Woman was spinning her web, spinning, spinning, spinning and she never knew when to stop. One day the web broke into a thousand threads and each thread she had spun had the power of retaliation in it.

One thread after another began shouting, "Who created this trapped mesh I am falling into?" "Not I," said the first voice, and on and on it went until the last thread had spoken. No one would claim ownership that they were the culprit and because of it Spider Woman got trampled over by the many voices inside her.

Even God had disappeared from the scene and all that remained was a crumpled heap. As much as God wanted to speak it was not the time for consoling her.

Up to now, Spider Woman had put up a good front and the mosaic she had presented to the world had value, but not enough value to save her from this downward slide.

Falling apart in front of everyone, her speech became garbled and she spoke in half sentences. Not wanting to reveal her past history to anyone, she became mute, tongue-tied, in front of an audience that applauded sophistication.

Dismissed as a nobody, Spider Woman could feel a new fire raging in her. It wasn't the toasty, warm kind you dip your feet into. Instead it took on the shape of a monster, red, hot and ugly. It was not the usual face she had been accustomed to and, yet, it was her face that had become distorted through the years.

The burning seemed to last for decades and not until Spider Woman received a good dowsing did the fire go out.

Then came Illumination with a lit candle in her hand. "Is this what you've been looking for?" she enquired. Sheepishly, Spider Woman gazed into the eyes of Illumination and said, "Yes, I was searching for the light but not until you came could I find it."

From then on, Illumination and Spider Woman became the best of friends. Wherever Illumination travelled, Spider Woman went with her. Sometimes in the darkest corners they would find other souls searching for the light and when it was their time the gift would be passed on.

WOMAN ALIVE

On the torn page
of a woman's book
the inscription reads:
"How can you say sugar is sweet
when you give me
spineless jelly beans?"

It's like saying:
"Keep me
in the locked cupboard
of your superficiality
and I will grow forever."

"Can't you see
how tasteless
I will become
or are you blind
to the marrow in me?"

Putting all this aside,
sometimes
a woman's emergence
is like that.
You say to the demon in you,
"Up now
and live
and you do live!"

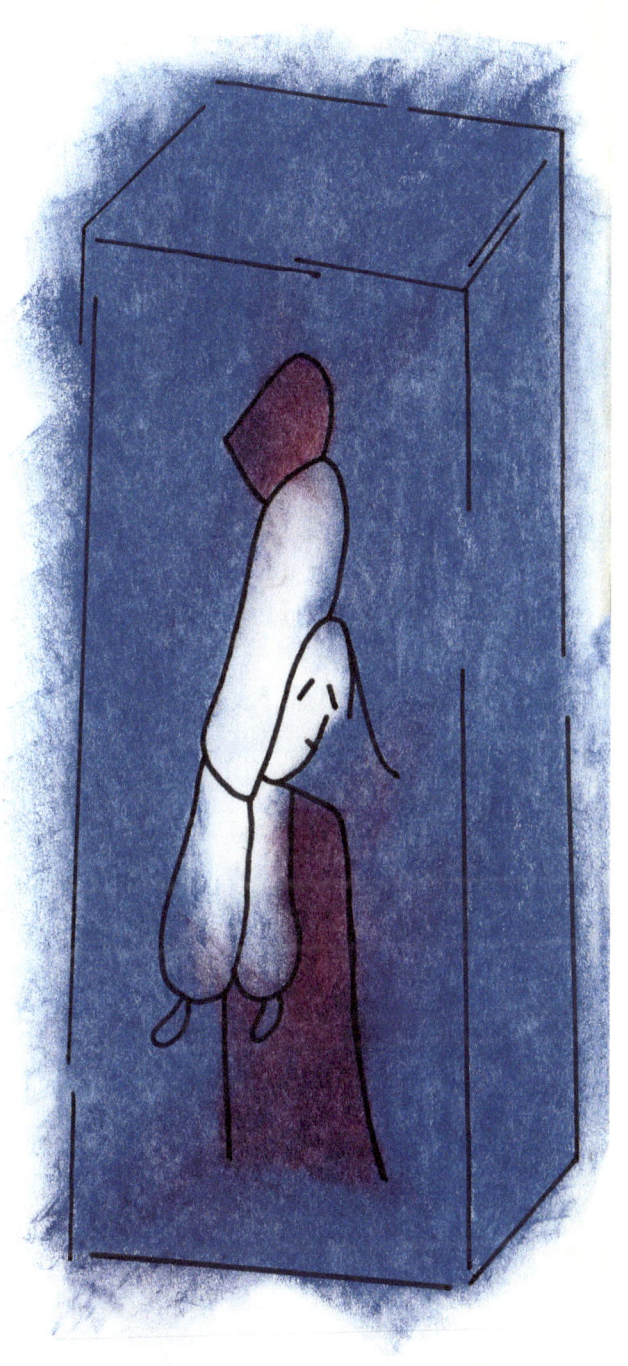

WOMAN ALIVE

Woman Alive came out of the cockpit singing. This time she was sitting in the driver's seat headed in the direction of wherever the Pilot would lead.

Suddenly, the plane shifted gears and she was no longer sitting in a place of honour. Unseen forces had taken over and a destiny that was once predictable was no longer so.

Up to now, she had been travelling in a human body that wanted to fly. Why her vehicle came to a halt was beyond her. She was young, vigorous and full of purpose and, yet, in her naivety there was one thing missing. No one had told her that for a vehicle to run smoothly it must be gassed up when the tank runs dry.

Inside her body, Woman Alive could feel the discomfort of a tank run dry and detested the new location she had been whirled into. Distraught and disillusioned, she momentarily lost sight of the Pilot.

Perhaps this is what Woman Alive needed, a shocked landing, so that any remaining traces of smugness would be taken from her. Striving to remain alive, she hated, not the Pilot, but the breath that was being taken from her.

Agonizing over her loss, she cried out, but the Pilot was nowhere to be found. Falling into a deep ravine, she could see off in the distance the higher altitudes the Pilot had lured her into. It was beautiful there and in her memory she could still feel the elation of it.

The soul of Woman Alive knew that her time had come. The Pilot had warned her that it wouldn't be easy. The terrain was rough, hard and steep. The choice was hers and whether she would follow remained to be seen.

Standing at the edge of her being, she could see ethereal faces in the distance urging her to let go and take the leap to where the air gets rarefied.

The remaining question was: Could she, Woman Alive, develop a new lung capacity to climb out of the ravine she had fallen into? And if she fell again would she still have the resilience to keep going?

Of course, no one had the answer for her, but Woman Alive knew in the depth of her being that she could and would do it!

GENTLE STRUM

Once sorrow
has plucked you
a home
your heart will sing
even as the lyre does.

If you run far from her
she will chase you
up a hill
put a ring on your finger
and say
marry me.

Only then
can Love
tilt your toes upward
spin you forward
into the pivotal dance
you came for.

Make sorrow
your melody
and she
will sing to you.

GENTLE STRUM

Gentle Strum grew up in a land called sorrow. Her parents loved her dearly but no one could satisfy the inner longing of this child until one day a cat came to live in their home, a kind, black cat with dark, knowing eyes. Gentle Strum named her Melancholy and they became best friends.

Each day Gentle Strum would sing her lyrics to Melancholy. No words were spoken but the soft, soothing purr of Melancholy was enough to send Gentle Strum into a land far away. As much as she tried to grasp what this exotic feeling was, Gentle Strum could never fully explain it.

As Gentle Strum grew older, her peculiarities became more pronounced. On the outside, she appeared normal, but on the inside she was definitely not your usual commodity. Sometimes you could hear her blubbering: "Too many possessions make me limp. They're like useless frills on the bonnet of my hat. Fussy creatures that leave me irritable on the inside."

Living in a materialistic world, Gentle Strum soon discovered how smothering that could be. She liked things but the accumulation of them would drive her into a tizzy and sometimes you would find her soul sitting on the branch of a tree.

Gentle Strum was not only a conundrum to herself but to the whole world. As much as she loved people and things, she needed a space where she could breathe in the taste of God, without the surrounding clutter hemming her in.

Melancholy seemed to understand and followed her wherever she went. One day Melancholy wanted to be alone and wandered away into a large carpeted area of the forest. She lay down near the trunk of a tree and died quietly and peacefully.

On finding her, Gentle Strum could hardly bear the pain of it and, yet, when she touched the body of her friend, she could feel the ache in her own heart lifting.

Perhaps Melancholy was a disciple of Jesus and now it was Gentle Strum's turn to do the same. Where this notion came from, Gentle Strum wasn't exactly sure, but what she did know was that the soft purr of God was growing bigger and bigger in her.

From then on, Gentle Strum could never get a big enough dose of love. Each time God filled her cup, she drank heavily and there was always room for more.

NAKED LOVE

When fever
broke
thermometer said,
"Undress yourself
because if you don't
Love will."

Without clothes
naked soul
lay shivering
in the dark.

Love
came close enough
to dismantle her,
gave her
a new heat body
that only
she could bear.

More pliable now
the pores
in her body opened
and she could feel
as never before
the warmth of God's skin
against her skin.

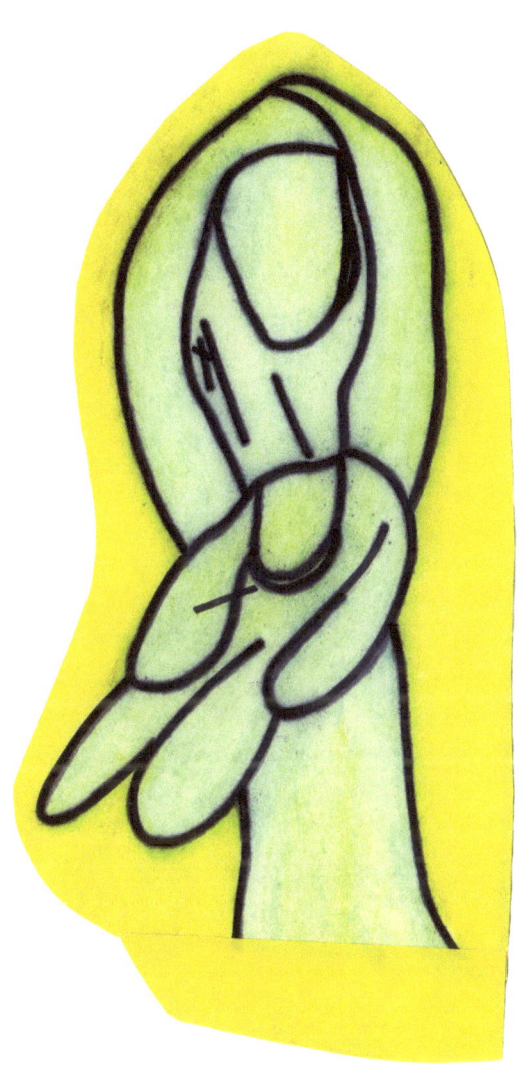

NAKED LOVE

Mother Love was about to make an announcement at the nearest radio station she could find. It was in honour of the daughter she had given birth to. She had named her daughter Naked Love because of the purity that was in her. It was an unusual birth, not the kind that happens in wedlock.

Even the news reporters trembled when the energy of Mother Love came near. They placed barricades all around her but nothing could stop the force of her entry. Then came the daughter, Naked Love, who was equally forceful.

Mother Love was the first to speak and out of the microphone came a clean, smooth sound from a higher realm. There was an untouchable majesty in her voice that was strong, bold and deliberate. "I have come to enliven and make you new," she said. "Where I want to take you, be assured there are no lounging chairs for the work that is yours to do."

The next at the podium was Naked Love, a woman well on in years, not the small frail child the news reporters expected. When Naked Love spoke, the ground shook from under her. "What can be more shocking," she said, "than returning to the womb for the rebirthing of a Power of Someone stronger and wiser than you are, for a fullness of Life you never thought you had the push for."

The room became instantly silent. Mother Love and Naked Love were the first to leave. The speechless reporters failed to announce the usual suicides, murders, bombings and killings of the day. Others left quietly, as if in a fog, as to what truly had transpired.

A year later there was an uproar in the city. Supposedly, nothing had changed and, yet, everything had a different look and feel.

Even the stray pigeons eating the leftover crumbs on the street seemed to know not to place their hope in a world where temporal things would soon disappear.

As for the people? Well, you could say there was a new yearning for even a mouthful of what Mother Love and Naked Love had left behind. Perhaps it would take another generation to get there but they were well on their way.

SOUL FIRE

Pregnant soul
you are more
than a body
without windows
you are a house
that sweeps itself
clean.

Held captive
by no one
you come out
the back door
of a prison
dancing
free!

You are
the flaming torch
the Energy
of the untouchable
touchable God.

On a blind slate
you open
our closed eyes
so we can see.

SOUL FIRE

Soul Fire spits out false food, has a dragon in her that sits down at a table and devours only true ingredients. Being young and naive, she chooses to live in an abandoned old house with a rickety top floor overlooking the ocean. So far, she's convinced herself that she's a spiritual being and on drab days, says, "Sun, come out," and Sun does.

What Soul Fire doesn't know is that if you deviate from truth, Sun can scorch you, can turn your white shirt black. Having been burnt once too often, Soul Fire was quick to learn that if your heart is clean, Sun would warm you with her violet rays but play the duplicity game and she would slap you hard.

As time went on, Soul Fire felt caged in and needed to satisfy her appetite for other delicacies that she somehow felt Sun was not revealing to her. When Sun wasn't looking, Soul Fire would deviate, go down rough patches of earth that often got her into trouble. She was definitely sincere but her detoured living caused her to get burnt often and she had a way of hiding the scars should people think less of her.

With a false sense of pride, Soul Fire reversed the student role and became the teacher. Unknowingly, she erected a tall wall of self-righteousness around her. Nobody could get in because she walled everybody out. Even her best friend got treated shabbily. "Go away, Sun," she would say and Sun did just that.

Much later and after repeated falls, Soul Fire held up a mirror to her face. With unclean eyes, the kind you want to pluck out, she sensed at some deep level what Pilate must have felt when he said to Jesus, "What is Truth?" and then with a rusty cloth washed his dirty hands clean.

Soul Fire wondered if she was a modern day Pilate that could just as easily be burned at the stake or was she a Joan of Arc standing on innocent ground? As she scrutinized her motives, she felt most probably she was a bit of both.

Whoever she was, she knew that the sin of the ages was in her too. "Oh, Sun," she cried out, "Come back to me!" And Sun rushed toward her with the same kind of violet rays that had so long ago soothed and warmed her. In a small clear voice, Soul Fire said: "Wash me thoroughly clean," and with that her eyes were opened.

RISEN ONE

Waking up
from my own concrete
I find you
in the most unusual places –
your hand
pushing through
the impervious layer
of a blockade.

Your foot
loosening itself
from the metallic chain
of a pedal
going nowhere
with the seasons.

More portable now
you could be above
or below the land
digging flowers
from the clay
of an unknown climate.

Wherever you are
the land has shifted
terrains are different
extinct perhaps
to those
who have not climbed
high enough.

RISEN ONE

Risen One was an ancient soul who had been hidden in a tiny crevice of the earth for too long now. Deprived of water and hidden away from the world, no one saw or even suspected how the earth's clay had hardened around her.

In this underground world, Risen One often wondered about earth's evolution and even asked her Creator if she could be part of it. Quite to her surprise, Creator responded with an immediate "yes", put a shovel in her hand and said, "Now, it's up to you."

Full of fatigue and pushing hard through the subsoil, Risen One was determined to become part of a new generation of awakened souls. Totally dependent on her Creator for guidance, she knew it had taken centuries to build the old world and what remained of its remnants, even that was crumbling under her feet.

"Where to now?" she asked her Creator and that's when the shovel was taken from her and placed in a ditch that had water in it. "It's muddy in there," said Risen One. "That's because you're trying too hard," said Creator. "Leave the foundation to me and I will build the rest."

Risen One was no longer in control. In the past, resistance had shielded her, had made her remote and small and even though she knew the size and shape of the land, it didn't allow for anything bigger.

This time Creator shoved her off the pedestal she had spent a lifetime building and said, "Make a new home for yourself with me walking in it."

Breathing more easily and deeply now, Risen One could feel the nuances of a landscape that was breathtakingly beautiful and far more rewarding than any of her former dwellings.

All around her now other ancient souls were doing the same thing, surfacing from underground. Risen One could feel a new momentum as the assembly line of ancient souls grew larger and larger. It seemed as if a universal uprising of great majesty and splendour was already occurring and nothing could stop its passage.

Remaining somewhat of a mystery to the larger world, Creator God, Risen One and all the other risen ones somehow knew that from now on they would be intertwined in a life and in a destiny whose unstoppable Energy would just go on creating itself.

WATER JUG

Surprised
aren't you
that the strained
out soul
at the bottom
of an ocean
is you!

Drowning yourself
to make yourself whole
is a ridiculous concept
and, yet,
there's an unstoppable
fresh current
in it.

It's no different
than purified water
leaking through
the bottom of a sieve.
It makes me ask
what kind of liquid
am I made of?

When this happens
I can't get enough
of God.
Casting my gaze
upon her
I can never quite quench
the thirst I feel.

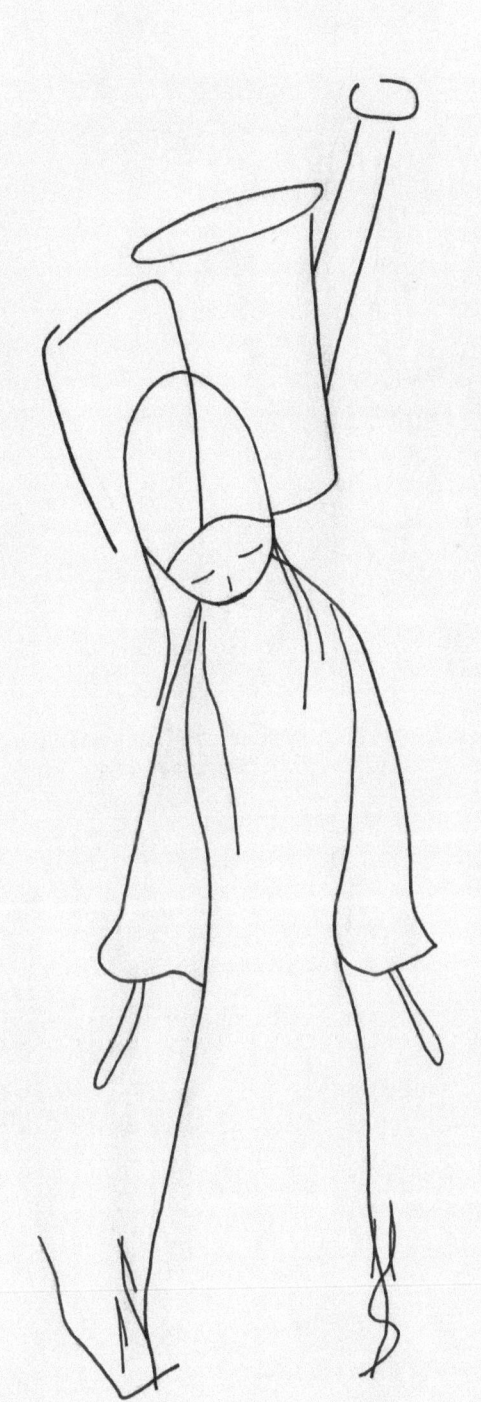

WATER JUG

Water Jug's first, last and middle name was thirsty. As a young girl growing up, she played the game called pretend. She was like a china doll, beautifully dressed up but not real.

Whenever Water Jug arrived at a place called desolate, she would pretend the ground was fertile. As much as she wanted to bathe in clean water, hiding her feelings was like living with a soiled faucet you can't turn off. Denial was an inbuilt habitual pattern that most probably began when she began.

As a young girl, Water Jug longed for companionship but no one could get in except for God who sometimes pushed the door open. Surprisingly enough, in moments like this, the barricade she had built around herself would instantly dissolve in a puddle of tears.

One day, God came disguised as Mother Nature and tricked her, lured her into a true way of being, and said, "You must shed the false skin of your former self because if you don't an avalanche will."

She was nineteen at the time and when the snow melted she discovered a stream running through her that seemed so easy to access. It was the first time a waterfall of such magnitude had visited her and she thought it would last forever.

She loved the new wardrobe of her soul. It was the exact right fit and even her clothes seemed to dance with an aliveness that bordered on ecstasy.

As much as Water Jug wanted to stay here, her dream world soon ended. Falling off her pedestal and stripped of her finery, she lost all semblance of direction. Plunged into the darkest of the dark worlds, death came as an intruder, squelching the Life Force out of her.

Years later, Mother Nature revisited her and said, "Water Jug, you are older now and ready for the truth. To have stayed at the waterfall would have been to stagnate. To keep the water flowing, you must leave the familiar shore and sail with me out into the deep. Only then will that dry, parched-out tongue of yours be satisfied."

With a sweep of clean air flowing through her, Water Jug looked lovingly at Mother Nature, thanked her for her wise advice and said, "From now on even a trickle of water will be worth the relishing."

FLOATING FREE

Smothered face
under the hood
you carry
your grief well
but it's time
to come out now.

A bent stick
leaning over
a crossbar
is what
you leave behind.

No hands
no feet
to steer you now
you could be
a pulley
in the wind.

Or more likely
a loose string
floating free
above the earth
air born
for this hour
of becoming.

FLOATING FREE

Life was a chess board, so exacting in its rules, that Floating Free could no longer endure the hardship of it. Deep down in the tavern of her soul there was no wine to drink, just an empty vessel crying out, "Why keep playing a game that defeats me every time I play it?"

As much as Floating Free hated losing the game and hearing the word "checkmate" over and over, she was still wooed by the Voice that uttered her defeat.

Sometimes she would name this nebulous Voice, Spirit, and then proceed to put a latch on her tongue for fear Spirit would speak.

Fear, like ignorance, soon placed Floating Free in an arena of despair, where she was quick to learn that if anyone didn't want to be jailed up it was Spirit.

Spirit had a wild side to her and didn't like being bottled up. Floating Free knew this when she first felt the slap of Spirit's wing upon her. Even though Floating Free was not always congenial with Spirit, what she did like about her was that She would have nothing to do with theologians who categorized her by placing a gender on her.

Spirit was the first to insist that because of her Infinite nature she couldn't be contained in a body and that there would never be a routine way of defining her.

At best, Spirit was an indefinable Mystery that would go on teasing the human family for decades to come.

Still somewhat ignorant of spiritual progress, Floating Free put a wig on her head and said to Spirit, "I'm a woman now and will let you mother me into wholeness."

This is what Spirit had been waiting for. With this kind of an invitation, Spirit lit up a match and breathed fire into her. With nothing remaining but a trail of black ashes on her tongue, it was not the holocaust Floating Free had anticipated and, yet, the Light blazing through her was the price she was willing to pay.

Wigless now, Floating Free had nothing to hide. The barricades were down and the clean echo of truth could be heard throughout the land.

Even if no one else heard, Floating Free heard, as if for the first time, her own hollow voice in the wind and she grew to love it as her own. On that day, she and Spirit were one.

JOYFUL PILGRIM

Fallacy
resting
in your cloistered
shut down pilgrim's heart
is no different than truth
sitting on a wobbly bench.

Now tell it as it is
your body undid itself
threw a tantrum
over the unlit candle
of your soul.

If joy
could be measured now
you would say
squashed down
deep down
into a pulp
is me.

I am the new flesh
of the ground-out one
know me
as I am.

A stone wall
bursting herself open
is how
I came to be.

JOYFUL PILGRIM

Joyful Pilgrim had the capacity to soar but her premature wings often collided with obstacles that pushed her off course. Owning that she was a slow learner was a difficult lesson and as much as she wanted to harness the Wind, the Wind had a way of harnessing her.

Belonging to a family of expert flyers, she had a secret yearning to one day fly higher than the others but, of course, this kind of thinking always led to her downfall.

Learning to fly was a slow process and each time she experienced defeat she came to understand better that pride is a peacock that sits on a fence apart from others.

As much as she disliked the experience of failure, her brittle wings were softening under the influence of it. There were even days now when she could glide through the sky with a strange kind of rhythm that felt right for her. Perhaps, too, it was the aging process that had mellowed her for the new climb that lay ahead.

Already she could feel the change happening. Something akin to air was stirring in her and out of her small bird-like frame came these majestic words:

"Humility is a small bird whizzing by you - a boy, a girl, a man, a woman, a cat, a dog, a tree, a flower, a twig, a shrub. Humility is being who you're meant to be."

No longer comparing herself to others, Joyful Pilgrim soon learned that there was enough space for everyone in God's sky.

If someone with clipped wings was flying at a lower level another handicapped bird would soon fly beside her and give her the assurance that all would be well. It was all part of the outreach program. In fact, being handicapped was not looked on as an affliction but a prerequisite for belonging to a family that would always care for its own.

For Joyful Pilgrim, this is what she had been looking for. Everyone was welcome here - big birds, little birds, fat birds, skinny birds. Black, yellow, orange, brown, there was no colour distinction made. Everyone, the young, the old, the middle aged, all were treated with the same kind of love and respect.

Looking around her now, Joyful Pilgrim was at home, feeling at one with her kin. "The whole of life is a school of learning," she said, "and nothing can replace the wonder of it."

ISOLATE BEAUTY

Silence
can swallow a whisper
instantly
can put a shield
over your voice
before you speak.

A tongue frozen in
on itself
knows this
you can't melt ice
before the mouth
is ready.

The body cries out
but the soul
silences her
says:
words
get manured over
ripen best in the dark.

Sitting
in fertile ground
if the soil aches
long enough
you will know beauty
when it seizes you.

ISOLATE BEAUTY

Living in a shut down building, herself lodged into herself, Isolate Beauty had a way of deceiving the medical world. She was not well and, yet, because of her outer sprightly appearance, a proper diagnosis never could be made.

She seemed to be living in two worlds, an earthly one where the strange ache in her chest remained just that - a hole in her heart that medically you couldn't stitch up.

The other world was where she flourished best. Sitting on the edge of a spiritual whirlpool, she could duck her head for days in these waters and always come out thriving, healthy and well.

Returning to the earth world, her soul was magnetically charged and she could light up a room by just being there. Her presence, though, always remained somewhat of an anomaly.

Trying to balance the two worlds was for Isolate Beauty like steering her car over a cliff before getting headed in the right direction and for that there were no medical experts. Not even the world of psychiatry could begin to touch her dilemma.

As much as Isolate Beauty needed help, she knew she was not a doctor. Being an explorer though, of her own destiny, she soon learned about her illness and how it could be treated. She wasn't particularly clever in an academic sense but when it came to spiritual emotional terminology she would soon become a master of her trade.

She was never overly religious but like a modern day Magdalene, she could wipe the feet of Jesus with her tears and feel totally at home in doing so. Jesus wasn't some distant being in the sky but somehow lived inside the anatomy of her soul breathing breath and life into all that had been injured.

Isolate Beauty finally found her footing and like a modern day Jesus of Nazareth applied for a master degree in the department of "Physician, heal yourself." There was no award for this kind of degree, just inner fulfillment that caused the lost parts of her soul to be reunited.

Deep down within her, Isolate Beauty could feel something stirring, a weight being lifted from her, and even if the Wind shifted or hurled her in another direction, she knew she would still be carried in the direction that Spirit intended.

TRANSFIGURED MISFIT

Embrace
your complexity
say to her:
a cobweb
hangs over
the left side
of your dismantled face.

She's the not well
part of you
the sagging fence
the teetering wall.
Grind her down
to nothing
demolish her quietly.

Then
with burnt feet
stand still in the fire
walk through it
to the no soot zone.

Now change your pose
and say:
that light
in the lantern
is you.

Become that flame
be brilliant
incandescent!

TRANSFIGURED MISFIT

As a young woman, Transfigured Misfit wore a veil over her head, face and body, a long robe that circled round her like a lattice fence. Peeking through the closed door of her smaller self, she was like a train without wheels, tooting her horn in all of the wrong places.

Bumping into other passengers on the tracks beside her, she soon discovered that lost souls have a way of gravitating toward one another. Finding her own clan, she soon learned that misfits aren't really misfits. They just travel differently without a map to guide them. Trusting life, it's as if the radar of Spirit gets inside them and propels them forward.

As much as Transfigured Misfit had found her clan, there was a streak of independence in her that set her apart. Often the pulse of her soul steered her in opposite directions to the tribe. Discerning if it was her ear or the ear of God that she was listening to sometimes got her into trouble. For Transfigured Misfit, though, trouble never remained trouble. She just saw it as a pit hole she had fallen into with a learning attached.

Divine schools were different than human ones. She liked them better because they taught you to risk the unknown path and there was never any blame attached. Just constant learning. To fall wasn't a bad thing. It just meant rising higher the next time.

Being open to the impossible becoming possible, Transfigured Misfit knew the journey would never end. Her train was headed toward Infinity and sometimes it would mean leaving the tracks to get there.

There was plenty of room on the train, seats for everyone. Outcasts, delinquents, everyone was welcome here. Whether any of her clan would follow was not for her to decide. Following one's destiny was a free choice and whatever direction individuals chose didn't really matter provided the ticket got them to where they were going.

For Transfigured Misfit, the ticket was not always pleasurable. Sometimes she would be travelling at a speed that was too fast for her and then the demonic spirit would leave a black stain on her soul. As poignant as this was, the pull of the great One was always there to rescue and save her from all that was unclean.

WIND-TOSSED FREEDOM

Rewrite
your destiny
and say:
Death
is a pen
you don't scribble with.

Scrape
the hem of her
and she will
swallow you whole.

With the breath
choked out of you
she's the ravenous Wind
inside your soul.

Sip life
from a narrow straw
and she will
diminish you.
Be shaken open
and she will widen
your territory.

Life
not death
is what
she feeds on.

WIND-TOSSED FREEDOM

Torn wing of a butterfly, that's how Wind-Tossed Freedom felt on the day of her birth. She came into our world with a stigma attached to her skin. Her brother's name was Jesus and he loved her just the way she was. "You're beautiful," he said, "glowing like a diamond and that's the way everyone needs to treat you." Wind-Tossed Freedom felt an instant connection with her brother and she knew they would be friends forever.

As she grew older her beauty faded and the stigma on her skin became more apparent. There was no sparkle in it. Nothing that would make her shine.

Even though she loved her brother and he was gone now, the memory of the glow and sparkle of the diamond remained with her. Hidden as it was in a tiny crevice of her being, she could still hear his words, "You are beautiful" and if no one else heard it she did.

Even on days and sometimes it meant months and years when the sun was gone from the sky, she could still hear her brother's voice from some distant realm. "My name is Jesus," he would say, "and yours is Diamond! Remember who you are and that will carry you through any storm. Even the worst pellets on the worst of days will not harm you."

Jesus always gave her courage, a strength that would lift her up when she had toppled down. For Wind-Tossed Freedom the love of Jesus was like having a battery inside her, recharging itself every time she became depleted.

Wind-Tossed Freedom never feared death. She just knew that the torn wing of a butterfly would sail through it when her hour came.

One day death approached her differently, secretly, like a lion pouncing on her prey. This time harsh teeth could have devoured her had not Jesus appeared on the scene with a whole tribe of modern day disciples who rescued her from the abyss she was falling into.

Wind-Tossed Freedom re-entered life and the diamond that had begun her earthly existence shone brighter than ever. Even her skin was translucent and whatever stigma had been attached to it was gone now. As for the torn wing of a butterfly, it remained just that, beautiful in its appearance and well loved by the owner of it.

CYCLONIC LOVER

Cyclonic motor
of a
whirlwind driver
get to know
the speed zone
of your mind.

If you haven't
smelt it yet
you soon will.

Burnt rubber
of a slit tire
on the road
will be the indicator
of your worst downfall yet.

Oust
all passengers
from your vehicle
yourself included.

From now on
drive carefully.
Remove the mask
of a charlatan
and toot your horn
inward.

The lit path
awaits you.

CYCLONIC LOVER

Inside her darkened mind, the whirlwind had already begun its devastation, but Cyclonic Lover did not know that. On an intellectual level, she was too young to know anything and, yet, on a spiritual level the script had already been written. Cyclonic Lover came into the world knowing where she came from.

Hardship would undoubtedly be a part of her destiny and, yet, her anatomy was such that she could bear anything. Attached to the soul of Cyclonic Lover was a small light bulb that never stopped glimmering. It was at the essence of her being and from early on she named it God. That was the part of herself that she loved best.

As she grew older, the world in which she lived became more and more an arena of hurt. Hiding her pain, she would squelch the tears that normal people shed but those same tears would come back to haunt her in the night.

Longing to make herself known, no one, not even Cyclonic Lover, could see the beauty in her jagged pearl, the one she held closest to her heart, the one sitting beside the light bulb in her soul.

As the years went on, Cyclonic Lover changed in size and shape. Losing her initial glimmer, not even her best friend, God, could reach the pocket of pus that had grown around her. Clever as she was, what she didn't know was that if a heart could explode, one day hers would.

On that day, the surprise of God came toward her and shifted everything she ever knew of life. The old house, the one she clung to, fell to the ground and in its place a spiritual mansion appeared.

Peoples of all races, creeds and colours were there. Most of them, like her, had been flattened by the drudge of life but here there was no more drudge, just an effortless way of being.

As much as Cyclonic Lover wanted to stay here her hour for return had come. She was not an electrician and, yet, her experience of the Divine was so charged with Light that you could have sworn she was an expert in her trade.

Her mission was to become an emissary of Light and not only herself but others too. Many had crossed over with her and having been consumed by the great Light knew that the Flame was eternal and could never be extinguished.

CARGO LIFTER

Too much static
on the radio
is no different
than refusing
to harness
your unruly emotions.

As long as you cling
to your ego
no amount
of knocking
on a shut door
will open it.

And, yet,
too much
heavy luggage
stuck
in the back seat
of a train
could be the nudge
pushing you forward.

Becoming a conductor
you must take
the lead role
shift gears
and put yourself
in the driver's seat.

CARGO LIFTER

Cargo Lifter had an impulsive side to her nature, flying high when her feet should have been grounded, walking slow when she should have been on the move. On the outside she appeared predictable but on the inside the chaos was beginning to show.

At times, Cargo Lifter was like a weathervane, whirling in all directions. Sunny, windy, cloudy, rainy. You could never tell how she was going to greet the day and, yet, she always presented herself as if the weather was clement.

Because the inward side of her soul was like a kaleidoscope, no one really came to know her as she was. "Hi, God," she would say. "The world is bright and colourful when you're in it." And, then, she would move into the duller parts of the city and say the same thing.

Of course, she was not welcome there. Anyone with a pollyanna personality, claiming that the world goes on singing when you should be tasting the grime, has not yet learned the advantages of the downside of life.

After awhile, even God became a foreigner

to Cargo Lifter, and that left her more confused than ever. In the dark of night when she was clinging to her kaleidoscope, you could hear her croaking at God as if she were some kind of a raven who had lost her way.

Unbeknown to Cargo Lifter, in the city where God lived, becoming lost was the prerequisite for being found. In her day to day living, she would now be plunged into a milieu of people that would at times disgruntle her. While some of the people were kind and respectful, others were obnoxious and placed on her path to teach her a lesson.

Bumping into the worst of the human family had a way of exposing her own gritty nature that up to now she had been able to camouflage. Living in the real world, Cargo Lifter soon learned that the field that needed the most ploughing was her own. She took to it diligently and came to realize that in the realm of God there would always be a new alphabet of learning. A to Z was for beginners and now Infinity wanted to expand her further.

Knowing all this, Cargo Lifter would never forget her initial kaleidoscope experience. It would always be there as a reminder of the first doorway into a God she could never stop loving.

NEW VISION

Freedom
is the name
of my balloon
and I go sailing
through the sky
with her.

In times
of turbulence
placing a life jacket
on me
when I resist You
creates havoc
in the water.

Dependent
on air
to keep me afloat
sometimes
I miss seeing You
at the parameters
of my being.

Oh God
of a hundred thousand
different faces
each time
you come close enough
to touch me
I get to name You
one more time.

NEW VISION

Picture a magnet moving at great speed with a woman called New Vision holding it. Like many other women of her time, she had come with a message and wanted to deliver it.

She was a small, diminutive woman whose feet barely touched the ground, and, yet, her energy was such that it could pull you in the direction she was going.

When New Vision was preparing herself for a meeting, she would first look at herself in the mirror, dress accordingly, and purposely place her glasses lopsided on her nose. That way she retained ownership of who she was and you could never be sure which way she was going to look at you.

At her gatherings, New Vision welcomed everyone. Retarded, brilliant, clean shaven, scruffy looking, it didn't matter who you were. You could be an intellectual genius or a stupid beggar on the street and she would still love and treat you equally.

On one occasion a scholar approached New Vision and said: "You simply don't get it. You treat everyone as if they had a degree. Even the poor person who hasn't had to work hard gets the same gold star from you as the one who has spent hours of labour getting his."

"Yes," said New Vision. "Your observation is accurate but what I detect in this poor person is no jealousy or enmity toward anyone, just love and self giving and that's how my school of learning is different than yours."

The scholar went off in a huff and New Vision soon discovered that there were many places where she was no longer welcome.

One day she entered a city of painters. It was called Truth City and they all welcomed her. The murals were fabulous and exposed how the truth of the people living there had made of their art something monumental. It reminded her of a modern day Jerusalem as fresh as if Jesus had just passed through.

New Vision sometimes wondered about the urgency of her own message and whether the genealogy of Jesus' skin was in her skin. Whatever it was, she somehow wanted the genealogy of that wheel to keep spinning. She was only a spoke in the wheel but already she had caught wind of its Fire, a Love so deeply embedded in her that it would go on burning forever and never let her rest completely.

SEASONED WOMAN

Like a fashionable dress
coming out
of a locked cupboard
you wear your dignity well.
Be mindful
of who you are
and dress accordingly.

When it's time
for spring attire
if you go looking for God
in a winter wardrobe
you may not find her.
She's the circuitous One
who could be wearing
a fur coat in summer.

Long before She was born
dictionaries
stopped defining her.

Still She comes
wrapped in diversity
the scrunched up
rake of Autumn
the leaf blower
dispersing you in shreds.

Leaning over a bent fence
She's the cushion
you rest your head upon.

SEASONED WOMAN

Red, yellow, orange, indigo blue, if you want colour in your life, Seasoned Woman will take you there. If you are ready, she will instruct you to jump into the limousine of your soul. With eyes closed, she will take you into the colourful world of the unknown. You will, of course, need your body to go there but more importantly your soul.

At first, it will be like dabbing paint on a canvass. Each person will do it differently and providing that no comparisons are made each soul will achieve uniquely what it came for.

Being a good instructor, Seasoned Woman will now stretch you a little further. "Take up your brushes," she will say, "and push them into the more murky colours. See what you find there and taste more deeply the shady side of the underworld where real life begins."

Some students for fear of losing what they had will want to leave their limousine behind. Others will embark on the adventure of splashing paint in all directions. Ceiling, floor, walls, wherever the paint lands will reveal the messiness of their new way of being.

Now comes the further test and not everyone in their limousine will follow. Seasoned Woman, having herself travelled into the land of the murky and far beyond, will now coax her beloved students into a deserted place called lethargy of the soul. Here, the paint thickens and becomes laborious with not even a trace of water to liquidize the hardened gobs.

This time her students will taste and feel how futile and colourless life can be. All accomplishments, any pictures they ever created will be momentarily forgotten, destroyed, laid to rest in a graveyard where only skeletons of their former selves appear.

Feeling the anguish and disillusionment of her students, Seasoned Woman knows the hour has come. She dismisses herself from the scene and takes on the role of an observant bystander. She's brought her students to the threshold and now it's her turn to step aside.

Each person must enter the gallery alone and say to the true Artist, "Does my work qualify?" Suddenly, the ceiling on the gallery will open and the entire tapestry of the person's life will be there, the good, the bad, the indifferent. Only then will the true Artist stand up and dab them all with gold.

CROSS CARRIER

Climb the ladder
to where you came from
and know this
a sluggish wheel
gets you going nowhere.

Stop putting
your foot on the axle
one step forward
means a somersault
backwards.

Go a little deeper now
spin your energy
inward
before going outward.

Remove the mask
of a hundred lifetimes
come out from hiding
and say to yourself,
cross carrier that you are,
if you're the abominable lion
tame her well.

Then take your face
to the mirror
and wash it clean.

CROSS CARRIER

Anyone meeting Cross Carrier on the street would have assumed by her demeanour that a wise soul was passing by. In her early years even she believed what the crowd was thinking. Naivety, of course, tricked her and sent her sweet smile into a dark cavern where the true teaching would begin. Pouting about her past or present situation was unacceptable here.

As a young woman, getting into the psyche of her mind was difficult because Cross Carrier had a sneaky way of barring others out. Her illness was so subtle that an outside observer looking in could totally miss the reality of what was taking place. This strange illness of not being wanted, not being seen, was sufficient ammunition to drive her and everyone else insane.

Perhaps her malady started in early childhood where she already knew that it was in her genes to heal. Who really knows? Maybe she was carrying the unhealed traits of her ancestors and was some kind of a prophet come to redeem herself and others. Of course, no one really knows when it comes to the world of speculation as to where the true answer lies.

Setting all this aside, the day came when Cross Carrier took hold of her true power. This time she knew she would not be deceived. The time had come and the journey was hers.

Admitting to herself that depression was a grimy place to be in was perhaps the first step forward in her recovery. In this dismal place, she often wondered where her spark had gone and had she really lost her soul or was she just imagining it?

On dull days, you could still see her trying to hide her pain. No one could pacify her. The wrenching went too deep. Even creation was a drudge. Nothing spoke or sang to her anymore. Cross Carrier wanted to die, "but not this kind of a death," she said. If she had known God's love at one time, she couldn't be sure of it now.

After the darkest part of the dark season was over, a glimmer of light shone through. It was early Spring and the day was partly dismal. All days had been dismal until now. Drifting down to meet her, a yellow butterfly rested on her shoulder. It was her left shoulder, the feminine side of her body, the place in her that needed healing. Life filtered through at the roots and Cross Carrier knew that in the sweet essence of her being she was alive again.

GRACIOUS GARDENER

Inside
my shoes
weeds wither
and I walk
out of them
barefoot
on the ground.

Shaking
the dust off me
my soiled footprints
need
no signature
to tell you
who I am.

Wide awake
in a sleeping world
my grubby hands
get smeared over
seeds
tumble from them.

Green grass
swishing
between my toes
wherever I go
the garden
gets planted.

GRACIOUS GARDENER

Whether the soil be soft, hard, moist or crumbly, makes no difference to Gracious Gardener. She's lived long enough to know all about acclimatization, how it can affect your moving forward or going backward.

When weather conditions are good, she knows you will most probably find yourself sailing along a smooth road with minimal interruptions. In that favourable season, you could be living in a land of luxury. Sitting in the garden of your choice, you could be a wild rose or sweet pea giving off a fragrance delectable enough for anyone to indulge in.

And, then again, a detour on the road could steer you in the opposite direction where you turn into something ordinary like a potato, pea or carrot. In this kind of a garden you could still find your worth. Hungry people would welcome you at their table and say how nutritious you've become.

If weather conditions worsen, you could, of course, be one of the soggy ones whose lettuce turns to mush. Even then Gracious Gardener will be there on top of the wet soil treating you royally as the king or queen of her garden.

Even though you've come to know Gracious Gardener as the benevolent one, there's another side to her, the more golden side, that will push you down before she pulls you up.

Gracious Gardener calls this deserted place, "Gethsemane in the trees." It's the darkest part in her garden where huge branches grind their way down into the mucky earth. As much as she would like to save her friends from this turmoil, she can't. And so, she lets them feed on their own gnarled roots.

Sometimes Gracious Gardener wishes that her friends would be quick learners but, unlike Jesus, they climb all the wrong trees before coming to the right one.

Infinitely patient with her fellow gardeners, the Gracious One says, "Have faith. Turn your face to the sun. Lie down with your clay body in it."

And then she reiterates, "Remember who you are. Taste again the rough turf of your body as if your bones were made of it. Only then will your tree ripen. Only then will compassion be the flesh within your body, the fruit within your soul."

HEALING RAINSTORM

Out in the rain
the drenched face
mirrors
the drip within.

Soul cries out
no more space
in the wet room
of my heart
no more space.

Down the road
from where I live
people mimic my grief
they weep
as if stones
know how to do that.

Emotions
die
on the ground
in front of them.
I swallow them
whole.

Tears
and then
the prick
of a knife
sobs me open
sobs me free.

HEALING RAINSTORM

In the big city people were rushing to prepare themselves for the worst blizzard of the century. Warning signs to abandon all homes and vehicles had been posted everywhere but Healing Rainstorm did not read them. Self-assured, she was an optimist who went glibly on her way.

Her horoscope reader had told her that the fortress in which she lived would one day collapse and even the news of that did not disturb her. Being too young to know about real tragedy, Healing Rainstorm put the reading aside until the painful day when she found herself sitting in an ice camp far away from her home of origin.

Lost in a gale of wind, snow and hail, the signs of disaster were all around and this time she could read them. If anything was going to rip the smile from Healing Rainstorm's face this would do it. Already, she could feel the pinch of pride upon her skin as people offered her a new form of lodging.

Other emotions surfaced too. Ignorance, grief, anger, with their ugly face of gloom. Shame that she wanted to hide in her back pocket. Defeat that would knock her down the stairs before she could climb back up. And even when her wicked strong-willed self stuck out its tongue she could feel the rock of her stubbornness crumbling into sand.

In spite of her violent emotions people were reaching out to her and this time when they offered her lodging she felt the freedom of a "yes, please" rising in her. Letting go of her former self, she could feel the hard clay softening.

As people came to know the other side of Healing Rainstorm they soon realized she was a unique soul who had been sent to earth on a pilgrimage that would one day make her special.

Waiting for that to happen was both an agony and ecstasy. People were telling her that she was travelling at a speed that was far too fast for her but Healing Rainstorm did not listen. She was like a car without wheels.

Finally, through utter and complete exhaustion, she put her small foot on the stop pedal and quite to her surprise her damaged body collided with her inmost soul. They became one as in a marriage. Body blessing soul and soul blessing body. This time Healing Rainstorm knew she had accomplished what she came for.

GLUTTONOUS LOVE

Small bird
dangling her mouth open
that's how she came to be.
Through the years
a strange swelling
the size of a dime
grew into something larger
than she could manage.

It was not about money
and, yet,
she was being eaten up
by a craving
that would soon devour her.
Hungry for love
and unseen by others
starvation became the heart
of the walled-in one.

Searching for air
a small trickle of it
sat down beside her
and said:
"You closed the window!
Now open it!"

A Breath
bigger than she was
scooted down
the back of her.

GLUTTONOUS LOVE

Gluttonous Love had a fastidious appetite. It wasn't for food but a craving that went far deeper than that. Inside her soul was an open wound that would fester night and day for Something outside of her, Something beyond space and time. As a young girl growing up she named it God but never spoke to anyone about it.

Most girls her age loved to play with dolls and often spoke about being a mommy when they would grow up. Gluttonous Love pretended to be happy playing their games but inside was a raw hole she could never quite get used to.

On the playground at school, she was a lonely child that would disappear from the others. Oblivious to her departure, no one came to find her but when the school bell rang she would amble in with the others, usually last in line.

Learning never came easy to Gluttonous Love. Her mind was always obsessed by how well the other students were doing. Stupid became a part of her everyday vocabulary but she never voiced it to anyone. Sitting in her desk at school she often became brain dead when others had the answers to questions faster than she could think them up.

Lethargic mind was all she could think of and that's the name she gave herself, a name that was far more derogatory than any teacher would have given her.

The drama continued right into her university years. Still sitting in a competitive seat where she knew she would always be the loser was something she never quite got used to.

Putting school and all else aside, Gluttonous Love was determined to make her way even if it meant being an outsider. Being less academic and more creative, she would often imagine herself being hoisted up on a rope that was long enough to reach this Someone greater and bigger than she was.

Even on the worst days when turmoil would come knocking at her door, it was as if Gluttonous Love had a magnet in her. So strong was this Love Force that it would hoist her up even when she was falling down.

Gluttonous Love went on to become a healer. What she so often craved came through on the Energy line and she named it, "God with her," the One who heals hearts that are broken.

SPIRITUAL REBIRTH

Say
to your overloaded brain
if words become nails
then it's time
to find your oasis
elsewhere.

Time
to loosen the knot
and unchain the chain
time
for the clogged mind
to travel lightly.

Be wise
about your future
the road you choose
will determine
where you're going.

If the butterfly
instinct
is in you
stop chasing
the woodpecker
up a tree.

Your wings
are too wide
to become small
again.

SPIRITUAL REBIRTH

Over the fence, over the wall, over all the pre-existing barricades, Spiritual Rebirth came bouncing to the finish line. Totally elated, but finding herself in a deserted village far away from the others, was a new and challenging experience for her who had left all to find all.

Feeling the tug of Spirit on her back, a ladder was placed before her, too steep she felt for a small person to climb. Resistant as she was, she found herself standing on the first rung of the ladder when the word abandonment appeared. Spirit informed her that she needed to taste and feel the strength of this new energy being pumped into her.

Bitter as it was, Spiritual Rebirth let the energy come in. Oblivious to what others might think, she drank it down and quite to her surprise found herself standing on rung two of the ladder. This time the word curiosity stood out in bold letters. Feeling the push to move forward, it was as if Spirit had already hooked her. Overly cautious by nature, she felt fear slide down her back into the great space beneath her feet.

Already she was on rung three of the ladder.

Spirit had captured her heart and she was up for the ride wherever it would take her.

Skipping to rung six, Spiritual Rebirth was applauded for her enthusiasm but was quickly pushed back to rung four when the word danger appeared in red capital letters. This time Spirit's Voice was loud like a siren and sterner than anything she had been accustomed to. "You're playing with fire!" Spirit said. "When you do that you'll get burnt and the torch you feel under you won't be pleasant."

One day Spirit caught her skipping from rung to rung. "What are you doing?" Spirit said. "Climbing to Infinity," said Spiritual Rebirth. "Isn't that where you live?" "Yes," said Spirit, "but you don't get there without me." Quickly losing her balance, Spiritual Rebirth slid back to where she started. "Ouch!" she said. "Too many slivers here. I don't like rung one. I've been there before and I don't like starting over again." Spirit applauded her for her great honesty and swept her back up to rung ten.

This time the sky widened and eagles flew overhead. Spiritual Rebirth and Spirit were in sync with each other. From now on neither would be trailing behind the other but together they would fly in the direction the wind was pointing.

NIGHT WATCH

Small moth
eating her way
into my cupboard
into the coat I wear
on special occasions.

Pretending to love me
she sits beside
the hole in my pocket
telling me I am food to her.
She's the enemy
against my skin
the one
who gets into
my wardrobe
before I do.

In my bed at night
I can feel
the flutter of her wings
all around me.

Tiny creature of God
if I am the giant
beside you
why do I fear you so?

Can I not
love you
the way you love me?

NIGHT WATCH

"God is everywhere," said Night Watch, "and sometimes where you see her best is in the dark." "Look at the stars," she would say. "They have faces that sparkle and the shining moon has a smile as broad as the sun." The night sky was a place of excitement for her and when she gazed up to the heavens there was so much brightness that she wanted to swallow it in.

As much as she liked the night sky, she was sometimes nervous in the dark and would stumble over her feet. As clumsy as she was, Night Watch somehow knew that God would always be there to pick her up.

During the daytime Night Watch could see God too. Plants, animals, trees, forests, oceans - God was everywhere and in people too. She could hear him in the drizzling rain, could touch, taste, feel and even smell him when the lilac season came round.

As she grew older, she became curious about who this God really was. Observing that God didn't have a mouth like hers, she enquired, "Are you a She, He, or It?" Of course, there were no words coming from God, only a strange kind of stillness that sucked her into something mysterious.

When this happened, she could have sworn that a warm blanket had been placed over her with an indescribable comfort she had never before experienced. Now she was really baffled as to who this God was, is, or would become.

Night Watch was older now and just an ordinary hard working woman. When each day was over, some observant people said they could see little windows inside the body of Night Watch. Night Watch knew they were there and said that was so God could peek in on her to see how she was doing.

After months and years of not seeing God, Night Watch wondered if a curfew had been placed upon her. Starved for God and the return of Love, she vacantly stared out of her little windows with only the squeak of a voice saying, "Does the diminishment of light mean that You are gone forever?"

This time it was as if God had a mouth with lips that wanted to kiss her. With God on her doorstep and unable to refrain herself from this kind of intimacy, she let her friend come in. Whether Night Watch would hanker after Love again still remained somewhat of a mystery. For now, she would simply bathe in this Love beyond all loves as if it were forever.

INWARD GAZE

Over the wrinkled forehead
and under the crooked chin
straight lines appeared.
This was the legacy
of a woman
who knew herself.

Speaking with authority
she said:
An unlived life
does not know
the zigzag road
until it gets there
nor does the woman
giving birth to her baby
know what awaits it.

So, too,
in all of our lives
we go out into the world
armoured
for the worst
and, then,
with the tick
of a heart beat
something gets crushed
within us.

INWARD GAZE

Being a woman, Inward Gaze could have given birth to a baby, but this time it was Divine Intelligence giving birth to her. Climbing into the womb of Divine Intelligence was restrictive and definitely not what she had planned on.

As a door to the outside world got shut, Inward Gaze didn't like the feeling of being cramped in. She decided to call Divine Intelligence "DI" which, in human terms, meant die, but in Divine terms meant live, and really live!

Divine Intelligence was concerned about the negative attitude Inward Gaze was developing and said, "I don't like the nickname you're giving me. It's far too colloquial and you need to respect my Presence more."

"Now you're getting bossy," said Inward Gaze, "and I don't like that either." Already a new awareness was growing between them and simultaneously they said, "Sometimes all it takes is a good quarrelling match to understand each other better."

Then came the next hard lesson for Inward Gaze. She wanted to know everything immediately and wasn't pleased when Divine Intelligence withdrew some pertinent celestial information from her. Feeling saddened and somewhat angry, Inward Gaze blurted out in a loud voice, "What does it take to become your friend?" "More pliability," said Divine Intelligence, "and a good dose of patience. Then and only then will you be ready to have your cup filled."

"As for your future journeying, you're still a young soul," said Divine Intelligence, "so it's back to the outside world you go, where inward becomes outward and outward becomes inward.

"In the outside world, you won't find me sleeping on a couch," said Divine Intelligence, "and you won't be there either. And, yet, when you return home at night, I assure you, I will be there to tuck you in. Travelling in my caravan will never be easy but it will get you where you want to go."

"Yes," said Inward Gaze, "I want to go." "Fine," said Divine Intelligence. "Is it agreed then that you will drink what I drink?" "Yes," said Inward Gaze as she gulped down a strong taste of the bitter and then indulged more fully on the sweet. Without further hesitation, she was on her way and the caravan was ready.

MESSAGE CARRIER

No one sees Spirit
but she does live
on the far side
of the wharf.
The further out you go
the more she sees you.

Noisy intellect knows this
and sits in a boat
steering herself home.

Already
she feels the warm sand
seeping into her
toes, feet, ankles, legs
her whole body unravels itself.

And then the push
of the shallow waters
returns her back to sea.

Spirit likens her
to a drifting log
and says:
It will take a swooping bird
or a broomstick chasing you
to awaken
that sleeping soul of yours.

Then, and only then,
will you fly.

MESSAGE CARRIER

Message Carrier wanted people's souls to sprout wings. Oh, how she wanted them to fly to the heights and depths of their being. "No more conformity," she would say. "Just be yourself. If your cup is already full, then flow like milk over a saucer. That way others can have a drink of you too."

Even though she wanted people to travel in the higher realm, Message Carrier knew it would often mean slipping back into a lower region. Sometimes there would be acid in the drink of the day and she would send out warning signals to her friends. "Be careful," she would caution. "Don't drink everything that on the outside looks good but on the inside is putrid."

Sometimes when Message Carrier would speak to her friends, she was not well received, like the day when she said, "Humans are most probably the next endangered species to go. They're no different than animals who can't defend themselves. Even Mother Earth is crying out in despair and few there are to hear."

It was time now for the great wake up, for the earth shattering moment to begin. The alarm had gone off several times before but this time people everywhere were scrambling for life. It was a modern day holocaust, a crucifixion of mammoth proportions reaching heights and depths beyond what Jesus could have endured. Innocent men, women and children were being slaughtered on the streets, gunned down and mutilated.

Message Carrier, who knew about Divine things, was horrified and felt that it might take another generation of withered trees laying down their branches alongside the tombs of these innocent people before something significant would happen.

Although she couldn't touch it, Message Carrier felt there would be a recharging of Divine Energy, a current passing through us that would give birth to a new generation of enlightened beings. Some were already here doing their work, she was certain of that, but soon others would appear too. They would arrive as lovers of the cosmos and out of the dead forest would come, not the withered trees of the past, but a new form of lush growth.

If Divinity had her way, and Message Carrier felt she did, from now on anything could be possible. Even a pendulum swinging backwards in the wind could be hurled forward if Love was the dynamism behind it.

AWAKENMENT

Before I began,
the footstep
of God
existed in me.

A small seed
just a sliver
of a thing
I was the tiniest
of the tiny ones.

A squawking
kicking
churning infant
Infinity
inscribed her name
upon me.

Another generation
is on its way now
and I tell her
outliving myself
is sometimes how I feel.

But she assures me
coming in
through the back
or front door
I will eventually
find my way.

AWAKENMENT

Awakenment addressed the crowd saying, "Can you imagine God sitting in a frenzy, giving birth to a child like me? Because if you can't, I can." It was Monday, the first day of the week, when Infinity, the mother of everything, took a deep breath in and said, "I am about to give birth to my first child. It might be something as large as the ocean or something smaller than a fish of the sea. Whatever it is, I know it will be good."

On Tuesday, the second day of the week, she gave out a loud roar. It was a child unlike any other and the universe rocked with glee. The child's feathers were soft as a dove and she floated over the thin air of morning. "I am eagle," she said. "I've been given wings to span the length of the sky. When people lose their way I will show them the route home."

On the third day, Awakenment was growing anxious and wondered when it would be her turn to be born. "It's Wednesday," she said, "and I'm still sitting in your womb." Being a curious child, she queried further, "How will I know when I'm being born? Will there be a period at the end of my name or capital letters in gold?"

Infinity laughed gently at the precocious child in her womb. "You'll know when it's your time," she said, "because your face will be no different than mine."

Thursday, the fourth day of the week, Infinity rose early. Awakenment could feel a strong movement in her, something like the force of a wind. Infinity's voice was softer than usual and she spoke to Awakenment the way a mother would speak to her newborn. "Come forth," she said. "Today is green day, earth day, and I have named it in honour of you." The love was so strong from Mother Infinity that Awakenment felt alive from the inside-out.

Now was the hour of Awakenment's becoming. Mother Infinity dropped her down, way down, into an imperfect world where she would meet other like-minded souls on a similar journey. Sometimes the path would be rigorous and would mean carrying the stigmata up a hill the way Jesus did, or on a day when the air was fresh and clean, it could mean soaring like an eagle through the sky.

Through it all, the world would be evolving, wondrously evolving, and Mother Infinity, full of her own mysterious wisdom, would always be there reminding her children to remain steadfast in their love.

THORNY BREAKTHROUGH

If grief
is the mouth of God
aching
to be born in you
why don't you
let her come in?

Is it because
venom
the thorn
in your cheek
dies slowly?

Or is it love
the warmth
of a jacket
you long for
but are deprived of?

Whatever it is
split
the bark open
chop the tree
down.

The breath
of God
cannot come
otherwise.

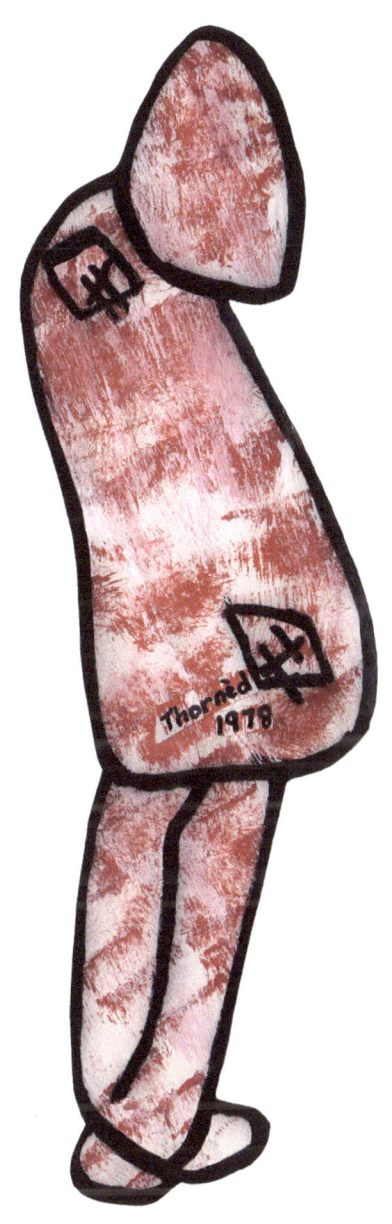

THORNY BREAKTHROUGH

Thorny Breakthrough knows that blood on anyone's jacket can discolour you for life. It can make you smaller if you wish or bigger if you choose. In the case of Thorny Breakthrough, throwing her stained jacket aside was never easy and, yet, it was the impetus that would one day make her fly.

As a small girl growing up, Thorny Breakthrough was shy, awkward and fearful. It took nothing to terrorize her. If someone looked at her the wrong way or spoke sharply to her she would shrink down to nothing. That's what happened on the first day of school. Something got squashed within her. Bossy children, bigger than she was teased her, and insensitive adults made fun of her small size too.

As the years went by, this lonely child with an orphaned heart smiled her way through everything. No one saw her and, yet, there she was at the end of a school day picking up the splintered pieces of her shattered heart. Highly sensitive and easily wounded, she was too proud to expose her injuries to anyone.

In the world of psychiatry, you might say she was a genius at hiding her pain. Children most often are, and adults too. But how was Thorny Breakthrough to know that?

In the drama of life, most probably there is a younger and older Thorny Breakthrough in all of us. We may not admit it but usually it's our own face, the disfigured one, we want to hide from. And, so, we create steel walls around our fenced-in egos until the fall of all falls becomes cataclysmic.

In the case of Thorny Breakthrough, she fell into an irretrievable ditch of her own making and someone other than herself had to haul her out. That's when Divine Spirit came in and washed the bruised part of her soul clean. There was no blood in this encounter, nothing that could ever shame her again.

Rising up, out of her blemished self, Thorny Breakthrough could feel at some deep level that the hour of soaring had come. She was not an expert in religious doctrine, not even a theologian, and yet, her experience and way of knowing God placed her in a category all her own.

Coming to know God from the inside-out, Thorny Breakthrough was able to say: "Only when you dig far enough down into the rubble will you find the gold you've been looking for."

QUIET TRIUMPH

Life
is a card game
shuffle the deck right
and the game goes on,
mix the cards haphazardly
and you're in trouble.

Hearts, spades,
diamonds, clubs
choosing one
over the other
is when
the wrestling begins.

If it's about
having favourites
then what's the point
of winning or losing
the game's already over.

Take a somersault
backwards
be surprised
and see what surfaces.

Triumphant love
written
on the face
of the joker
and it's yours
for the keeping.

QUIET TRIUMPH

"Centuries of people have come and gone," said Quiet Triumph, "and here we are today asking the same silly question of the historical Jesus. Will there be a second coming and, if so, what will it look like?"

It was then that a courageous modern day Judas stood up in the middle of the crowd and said, "I've been sleeping in my grave for 2000 years, chewing on my guilt, and now the hour has come for me never to disown anyone again."

Another modern day woman, who had raised her fifteen children with love, returned to the earth as Saint Teresa of Avila. She was a woman of her time who spoke eloquently. "The world is long overdue for an overhaul," she said. "Too many hierarchical rules that stifle the life out of a person must go. And go they did!"

Once more, Jesus of Nazareth came forth in the pure eyes of a 20th century dying woman. "I am so alive in the centre of my being," she said, "because in my essence, I have learned to let the Light shine through. Some people call me God while others say, I'm the Buddha of royal lineage. Whoever I am, I am Love incarnate."

Next came a speechless, newborn baby. Even disbelievers knelt down when the cry of innocence echoed through the room. It was the return of purity, dispersing all that was evil in us.

Finally, a long trail of brutal, fanatical leaders came forth with heads bowed down in shame. Genocide, the worst of all evils, was being acknowledged and forgiven. There was no other way for the second coming of Jesus to be heralded in.

As for Quiet Triumph, no further words were needed and, yet, the energy of gratitude that permeated the room spoke for itself. Quiet Triumph and the whole earth stood still. Everything became motionless except for the stars that seemed to blaze more brightly that night.

In front of everyone, the cosmos was giving birth to itself as God's love burst open all pettiness, all forms of malice and placed lamp stands in peoples' hearts so they could see.

Blindness was about to leave the earth and the new heaven for which we had been created was already on its way. When or how the completion of it would happen remained to be seen but each of us went away knowing we were part of its birthing.

WINTER BIRD

Feeling deflated
the way a balloon does
is a sure sign
that winter
is upon you.

Searching for light
betrayal
is the blind force
leading you down
a stairway
into the dark.

If your house
is no longer
a place of refuge
you must empty
the furniture in it.

Leave
the dirt windows
behind
and say to yourself,
"The sick bird
needs a doctor
to make her well."

Only then
will your clipped wings
fly again.

WINTER BIRD

Winter Bird came into our world as a premature entity living on the edge of nowhere and, yet, finding a place in every hemisphere of the globe. North, south, east, west, she would go in whatever direction the wind took her. Even though her wings were too broad for confinement, life had a way of dragging her down with it.

Right from the start, Winter Bird was embarking on a treacherous path. Hers was a destiny to rise and fall and fall again. That's when Spirit came into the picture. Of course, there would be many teachers along the way but Spirit would be the most unpredictable of them all.

Spirit's teaching was different than the others and Winter Bird, being an obstinate being, often said, "My way first," which usually meant disaster.

At school, Winter Bird had already learned, if you tell a dumb child perfection is the norm, she'll grow up believing it. Spirit, of course, wanted to shake Winter Bird out of her false belief system but Winter Bird was a slow learner and resistance is something she clung to.

One day the fog rolled in and Winter Bird admitted she couldn't see. "Oh," said Spirit, "are you ready to learn your lessons now?" Reluctantly, Winter Bird said, "Yes."

"Have you known anger?" said Spirit. "Of course not," said Winter Bird complacently. "I sleep with a lullaby in my heart." "Oh," said Spirit, "and when it turns into a nightmare, how do you account for that?"

Spirit was a disciplinarian and Winter Bird didn't like what she was hearing. "Truth," said Spirit, "is when you stop looking into the mirror sideways and see yourself as you truly are." "Ouch," said Winter Bird. "That hurts. I thought you were going to protect me from the ugly face of evil in our world."

As kind as Spirit was, she momentarily glared at Winter Bird, as if to say, "Wake up," and then she said it. "If that's what you think my mission is, to save you from evil, then you're wrong, Winter Bird. You must first be plunged into it and then you will learn what everyone learns. Evil is a part of shaping your destiny."

"Oh," said Winter Bird, "then take me on this expedition as far as I need to go." With that, Winter Bird's wings flapped rapidly, but never at a pace she couldn't manage.

SHEPHERD OF NOWHERE

God
is not the lost shepherd
hounding her sheep
you are.

Imagine now
a wayward soul
prowling through your room
at night
and say to her
that woman in disguise is me.

Taking ownership
for your name
everything will change.
Anonymity will be gone
and the shabby, outdated clothes
in your cupboard
will give way to the new.

As for the tarnished jewellery
people will discard it
and follow you
to your true destination.

Kneeling beside them
you will say:
"At my altar of betrayal
even a stone
shattered to the ground
gets to walk again."

SHEPHERD OF NOWHERE

Lost, always lost, Shepherd of Nowhere maintained that a small meadowlark lived inside her throat. From the moment of her birth, she somehow knew this unique bird was central to her identity. It was, in fact, her trademark. For astute people, they recognized her Song immediately and were drawn to the melodious quality of it.

Even though the hierarchical male birds disliked the fine-tuned quality of her voice, it was the feminine side of her nature that she clung to. Sometimes the energy of the "so called" superior group would lash out at her and her frail feathers would get torn and flattened.

When Shepherd of Nowhere sensed that the disapproval of the hierarchical birds was growing stronger, she chose to sing her Song quietly, out in the fields where the sheep went roaming.

Sometimes the hierarchical birds would peer over the fence with a sneering smile as if to say: "the mundane field is where you belong." Fluttering her wings and pretending not to notice them, Shepherd of Nowhere could still feel the poignancy of an arrow travelling through her.

Whenever this happened, the sheep roaming in the field would gather round her. Snuggling up to her, Shepherd of Nowhere could feel the warmth of their wool against her soft body and this was enough to induce the Song she had come to sing.

The hungry sheep, of course, were waiting for her melodious melody to stir the ground on which they stood. Once begun, no one could stop the music flowing from the throat of Shepherd of Nowhere, not even the hierarchical birds who wanted to fasten her wings backward when the only way she could go was forward.

Shepherd of Nowhere had travelled far enough into herself to know that once the true voice is captured by the owner of it, no one can take it from you.

Whether speaking to her sheep or the hierarchy, her message remained the same. "Male or female," she said, "it doesn't really matter who you are provided you sing the Song you came for."

Like an indelible mark upon her soul, Shepherd of Nowhere would from now on claim her birthright whether in the field or sitting midstream among the hierarchy. It was in her blood to do so.

PROPHETIC WORD

Your soul
is a compass
pointing inward
she speaks
without
being spoken to.

Perching herself
inside your suitcase
she says
travel lightly
shed everything
you don't need.

If it's worry you cling to
dispose of it
like scraps
in a waste basket.

Then
like a pea pod
crack yourself open
you must lose your voice
to find it.

Without sound
SILENCE
the unspoken
tipped over word
is what
you revel in.

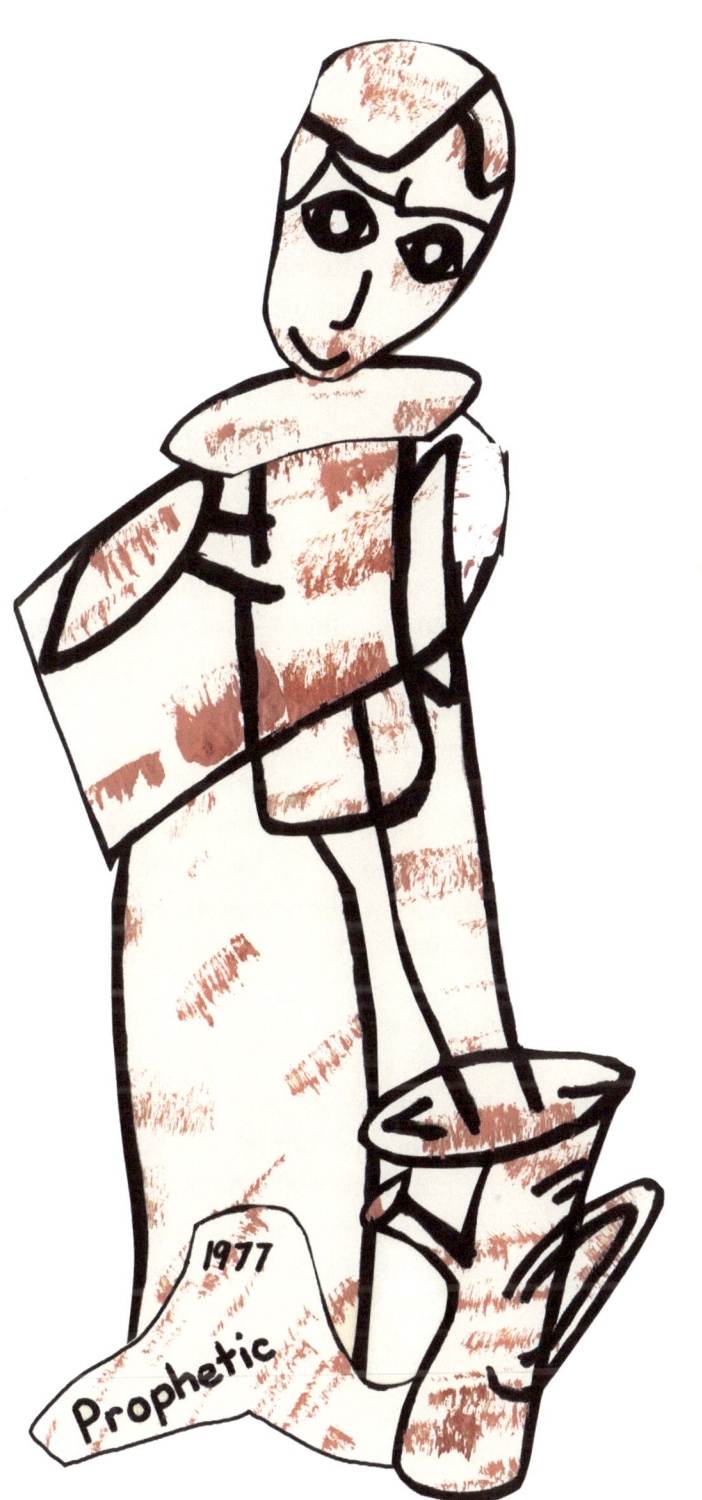

PROPHETIC WORD

Stretching deep down into herself it was not the first time Prophetic Word had dislocated her tongue nor would it be the last. Talking was something she was never good at and so she would say to her tongue, "Go to bed now." In other words, don't speak until you're spoken to.

As a small, shy girl and even as an awkward adolescent and sophisticated young woman, Prophetic Word could feel how deep her insignificance went. Trying to alleviate this problem she chose to be a stage performer. On the outside, she dressed herself in a stylish way and to all appearances came out as a finished product, perfect in every way. But on the inside her soul was playing havoc. Playing the game of pretend went on for years until the day when she smashed her mirror and said, "Ego be still!"

Prophetic Word was older now and knew with certainty that she was searching for something greater than she was. It was an enormous Something and initially she named it God, a Love Force that had the power to make the string on her yo-yo go up when everything was going well and down when the day turned gloomy.

The world of science told her it was just gravity she was playing with and, yet, she chose to dispute it. "Gravity," she said, "is the force that keeps my feet on the ground and has the name God attached to it. It's the Almighty Power that lets the string on my yo-yo rise above my mundane self and do magical things like pumping ethereal songs into me." She concluded by saying, "I may not be a Beethoven in this lifetime but who knows what the next may bring?"

Her soul was always evolving and nobody could stop the dynamism of it, not even the world of science and, yet, that world was evolving too. People were creating new things, some of them spectacular. Prophetic Word relished their discoveries and saw them as all part of the Eternal Plan, a mystery that had a way of making her yo-yo bounce even higher.

Even though some scientists negated her belief system she still spoke as a woman with authority. "Nobody has a claim on anything," she said. "We're all part of the great Mystery that will go on stretching us until the end of time or will there even be an end of time she questioned?"

That having been said, Prophetic Word remained silent and a strange hush filled the room.

ETERNAL WATERS

Inside my pitcher
the withdrawal of scum
grey scum
greasy scum
my scum.

Sitting
on the fringe
of my mind
exposing myself this way
black crow reminds me
her cawing
is no different than mine.

She's the irritant
inside my soul
making the pool clean.

Obstinate as I am
stepping into
a clogged stream
impurity
gets flushed out
of me.

Finding a clearing
it's taken a millennium
to harness
these waters
to where the river
now flows free.

ETERNAL WATERS

Right from the start, Eternal Waters was a lost soul searching for her identity. It was as if God pushed her into the world and said, "Learn to swim," but never gave her the boat or swimming apparel to go with it. Even on the day of her conception, when Divinity breathed fire into her, she felt lost, terribly lost.

Saying good-bye to the familiar, Eternal Waters soon found herself swimming around in the womb of her mother. At first, it was warm and cozy, a reassuring place for a foreign body like hers to be at home in but then came a strange thud as hard as a piece of wood. Her safe boat capsized and she was thrown onto shore, into the land of the living but somehow she knew people died here too.

As much as she wanted to exit her way back she knew it was not her time yet. Totally frightened and lost in a world that bewildered her, she was always anxiously looking for Something she could never find.

One day she spelt God's name backwards, (Dog), and said to the One she was groping for: "I feel like a dog that's been let off its leash and I have no one to lead me." God must have heard her because even though she didn't like being confined by a chain, she wanted some form of stability to guide her on her way and it wasn't the tyrant God she had sometimes heard about at Church. For her, God was far more soothing than that, something like a waterfall flowing into a stream.

At an early age, Eternal Waters was already balking the system in a quiet, underground sort of way. She had a gypsy spirit that caused her to wander off in directions that were not always good for her. She'd often get into murky waters and rather than have God pounce on her as a tyrant she would steer her own ship back to where the stream runs clean.

Nobody had to teach her anything, not even God, because failure she soon learned was the best teacher of all.

She was well into adulthood now and slowly, ever so slowly, she learned that the guiding Force who brought her to earth would return her on the day she was ready.

With that kind of assurance, Eternal Waters sailed freely, lovingly and willingly. The motion was always forward and into the deepest waters she could get to.

SUN WOMAN

It's all about
bursting your bubble
breaking through the froth
of what it means
to be real.

If night is what
you've been living in
tell it
to the dark face
of the moon.

Now look at the sun
sitting behind the cloud
if she ever spoke
the way you do
you'd be disheartened
by her.

Glimpsing
beyond
the narrow field
of your smaller self
push the closed door
open.

Unzipper
that zippered heart
of yours.
A warm house
is better than a cold one.

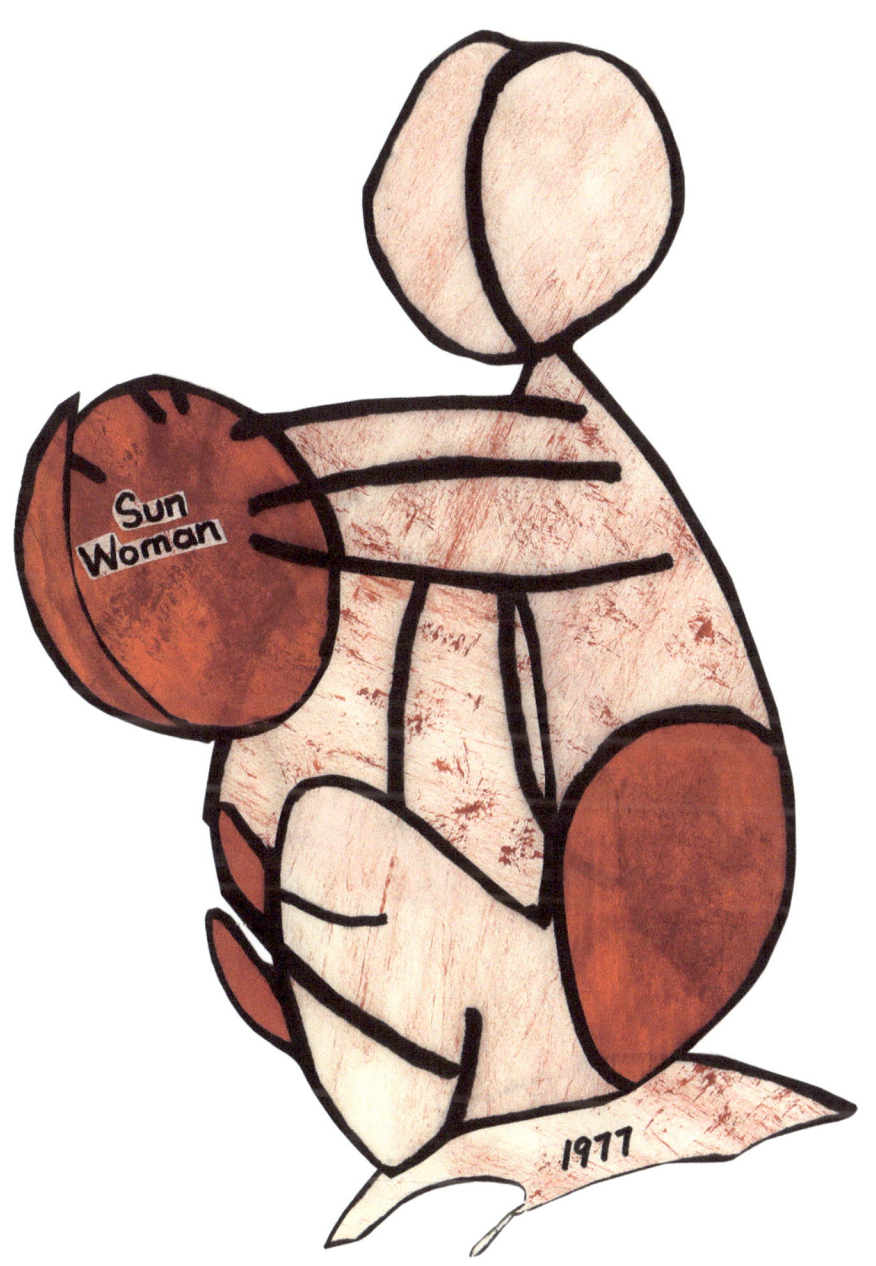

SUN WOMAN

Sun Woman has a warm, radiant face that glows in the dark. No longer a stranger to herself, she's met her enemies and told them to stand upright.

To fear, she says, "Stop cringing behind the door of the assembly room. Speak what needs to be spoken. A genuine voice is better than a ceramic one."

Next comes doubt, the one who never believed in herself. Dressed in some kind of foolish finery, Sun Woman says, "A puppet always a puppet," but then comes the real you and the world of disguises disappears forever.

Following behind is shame, always the last one in line. She has kind eyes but under the mask she's raging to be seen. It's late now and Sun Woman is approaching the end of day. "Know yourself," a Voice says, "and stop bumping into your own shadow. You'll sleep better that way," and so she does.

Next day, going down the path further, ugliness visits Sun Woman and says, "You've befriended me for too long now. Accept your framework as the only one worth living in," and with one last exasperated kiss she promises to do that.

Shortly after, vanity visits her. "You're now wearing a wig," she says. "Are you still trying to hide something?" This time, Sun Woman is totally embarrassed and blurts out, "Do you like it?" "No," comes the answer. "Your straggly brown hair suits you better. Learn to live in your own skin and see for yourself, people will love you just the way you are."

In the evening, liberation sits down beside her. "Sun Woman," he mutters, "do you know yourself now?" Only partially, admits Sun Woman, and tries to justify herself by saying, "Male and female are never what they should be. One is controlling and the other submissive." "Not so," says liberation. "You must be both. Be good to yourself and you will see."

Snuggling down for the night, liberation whispers a soft something in Sun Woman's ear. "You're beautiful," he says, "not because of your looks but because your soul has a bouncy freshness when you let acceptance come in through the door."

"Oh," said Sun Woman. "That must be why I feel the warmth coming into me now."

ASCENDED SOUL

Picture
the worst scenario
as being the best.
Death
slumped over a chair
is like that.

Aging
is not about
placing a torn rag
over your wrinkled face.
It's far more exuberant
than that.

It's letting go
of your appendages
feet, arms, legs, hands.
Awkward as it may be
you'll know the time
when it comes.

Rising up
or falling down
the welcome mat
will be there for you.

An empty tomb
torn open
is the way
your soul
leaves the body.

ASCENDED SOUL

When the veil momentarily got lifted, Ascended Soul knew she had experienced something profoundly beautiful, something Other-worldly. It was an alone trip where she had been transported, elevated beyond her normal way of living.

On returning to the earth plane, Ascended Soul knew she had been in a zone of transcendence and the illumination of it had already left its imprint. It was as if she had been given a third foot to walk with, and with that foot came a new kind of instinct that would lead her on her way.

How she got to see, touch, taste and feel this angelic realm, was beyond her fathoming. It was an enormous gift, totally unwarranted, and yet, graciously received. As she silently stood in the bliss of it, she knew her life would be changed forever.

As time went on, this transcendent realm and way of being would sometimes drift in and out of her subconscious mind. For Ascended Soul, it was like having visitors from the Other side come knocking at her door. Each time she let them in, the Light within her grew more visible.

But for now, the earth world would be her learning ground, the school she had chosen to live in. Sometimes her lessons would be difficult, and like a cup without water, she would often die of thirst. Seeing death marching toward her in this way was never pleasant but somehow she managed to survive.

One day the angelic realm came toward her and announced their arrival this way: "We are beings of Light, come to remind you that the veil between our worlds is paper thin. Each time you plug into our Energy, the enlightenment will come and you will do even greater things. The earth will be lifted up and you with it. Each of you will be hoisted up, hoisted into a world that has been transforming itself from the beginning of time."

Ascended Soul listened to the message of these wise elders and said to Jesus, the leader of the clan, "When it's my turn to jump through the net that has entangled me, will you be there to catch me?" "Not I alone," said Jesus, "but all those who work with me to raise up and make straight that which has been tangled." Breathing easily and deeply, Ascended Soul understood her journey now and became part of the team that would make her whole.

STILLNESS

At the dinner table
be careful
what you indulge in.
Sometimes speech
like luxurious food
goes down
the wrong way.

You say nothing
but somehow know
silence
is the medicine
of God's fork poking you.

It's the sharpened knife
of the crucified One
reminding you
that some things
are best left
unsaid.

Centuries later
you place the bread
of the risen One
on your tongue
as nourishment.

This time you know:
a silent heart
is a punctured heart
made whole.

STILLNESS

Stillness lived in a remote village away from the others. She was a contemplative soul who more than anything loved the quiet. Yet, deep within her anonymity was the mother/father instinct, not to raise a family of her own or to have children, but to comfort those in need.

Stillness had a dual personality, needing the quiet for restoral and the activity for fulfillment. Being true to her destiny was a long and hidden process that often meant being unbalanced. Over extension would tear her down, frazzle her out, and at times push her beyond her limits.

In turbulent times like this, it was difficult getting to know Stillness. One moment she would be warm and hospitable and the next she would be distancing herself from the crowd. Even her best friends sometimes mistook her need for survival and would send out a search warrant for her.

Whenever this happened they would find Stillness lying down in a field of roses with a subliminal fragrance all around her. Without having to speak a word, Stillness would look at them with a knowing glance that indicated she knew things from the inside-out.

Not fitting into the norm, the crowd would sometimes ridicule her but if anyone tried to dissuade her from speaking her truth, she would say: "The voice that whispers God knows where she came from."

With that kind of a pronouncement, Jesus the Nazarene suddenly stood beside her. "Don't be shy," he said. "Speak your truth. Say my name as if it were your name. Then turn the Bible over and listen to me."

Standing behind Stillness, even the hesitant crowd began to listen. Jesus lowered his eyes and said: "I came that you may have the same telescopic vision that is mine. You and everyone else before and after me is in the line of my lineage."

Looking directly at them now, he went on to say: "I am the timeless One telling you this: there's a Pilate and Judas in all of you and a Jesus too. You were at the Last Supper with me, so don't deny it! It's the dark side of humanity groping for the Light."

Finally the hour had come. Truth won out and the face of Jesus came in. Gazing at the Light, Stillness and the whole crowd uttered: "You struck us down to raise us up! You made us blind so we could see!"

FOREIGN DANCER

If you want fluid water
let the tears come
too much hardening
leaves a dint in your soul.

It's no different
for a child
soaking in bath water
one day
she'll grow up.

Her father says
take the slippery slope
first
you'll slide into life
easier that way.

But when your departure
is near at hand
don't let homesickness
be the cry
that detains you.

Just say to your mother
one foot
placed in a wobbly shoe
is better
than two feet
stranded
on the dance floor.

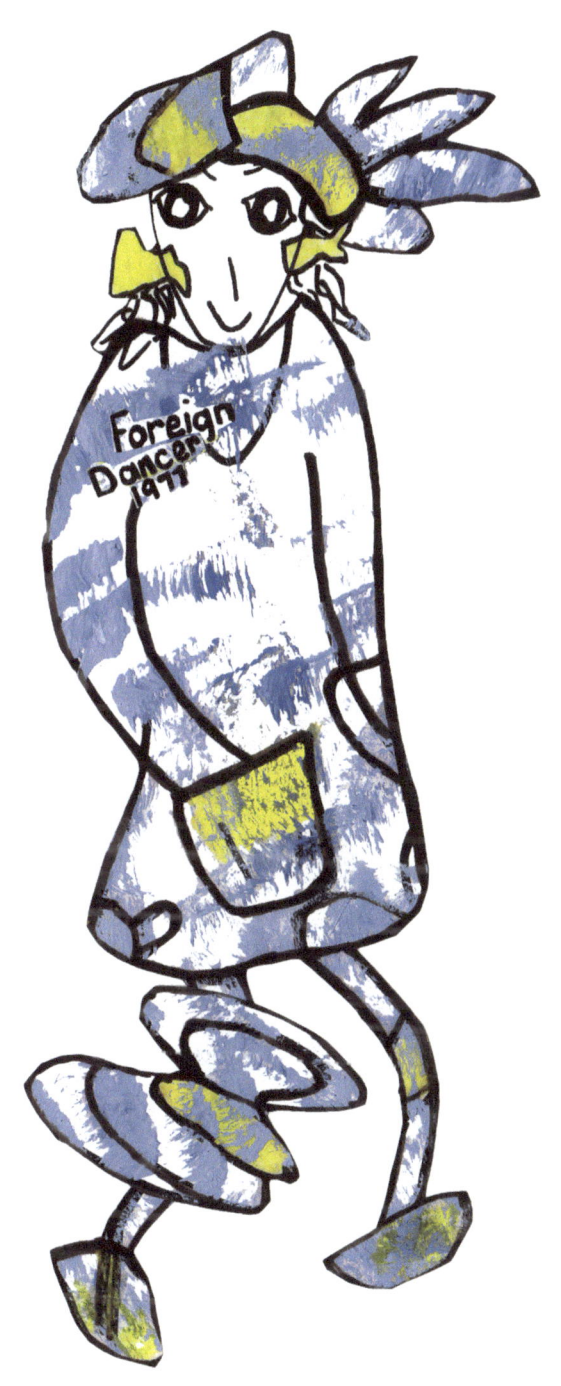

FOREIGN DANCER

With dark black eyes the colour of soot, Foreign Dancer had a penetrating gaze that seemed to say, "I know you." Some people feared to look at her directly for fear she would disclose too many secrets which was not her intent at all. In fact, if anyone came too close, she would distance herself saying, "Intimacy can be a dangerous thing when you don't know yourself."

Supposedly Foreign Dancer knew herself well but had no idea about the extent of her own flawed history. It was the good side of herself that she loved and rarely did she expose the darker side of her nature. She was a private person who maintained her distance for fear of being misjudged until the day when her bottled up emotions got the better of her.

Something was about to change. She could feel it coming and, yet, when it did come Foreign Dancer found it difficult to admit that the monster living in others had also taken up residence in her. There was an undercurrent of negativity disrupting in her. It was the aggressive side of her nature she could no longer sit on.

Up to now, sarcasm had never been a part of her nature but this time it was. "I've been on many dance floors," she said, "but never understood the lilt of my own feet until they were stamped on." That being said, she spat out anger and there was lots more to come.

Embarrassment, guilt and shame covered her pure white skin and left greasy marks over a smile that was no longer complacent. It was like going to a funeral, her own of course, and coming out on the other side clean.

Getting cracked open this way, Foreign Dancer quickly learned not to resist the process. "It will happen anyways," she said, "and it will allow people to see that being human and having negative emotions is all part of the process of making you whole."

Being vulnerable released her from the too heavy luggage she had been carrying. With self-acceptance and forgiveness in her bag, Foreign Dancer was free to go anywhere now. With this new self came a current of love and sorrow that ran rivulets through her. Quietly embracing herself, Foreign Dancer breathed deeply while placing both hands on her lungs as if to say, "It's the coming home journey I've been waiting for."

STRONGLY ROOTED

If your life becomes
an encyclopaedia
maybe you're on overload.
Try making it more succinct
a book with one chapter
instead of ten.

Now scrutinize your work
a script written
without a tear in the paper
tells only half your story.

That's why
a pencil
without an eraser
is the best way
to get to know yourself.

Mistakes
are the springboard
to knowledge
erase them
and you deny
your journey.

Ask yourself:
is your story
solidly rooted
or is it sitting
in a wheelchair
on the whim of another?

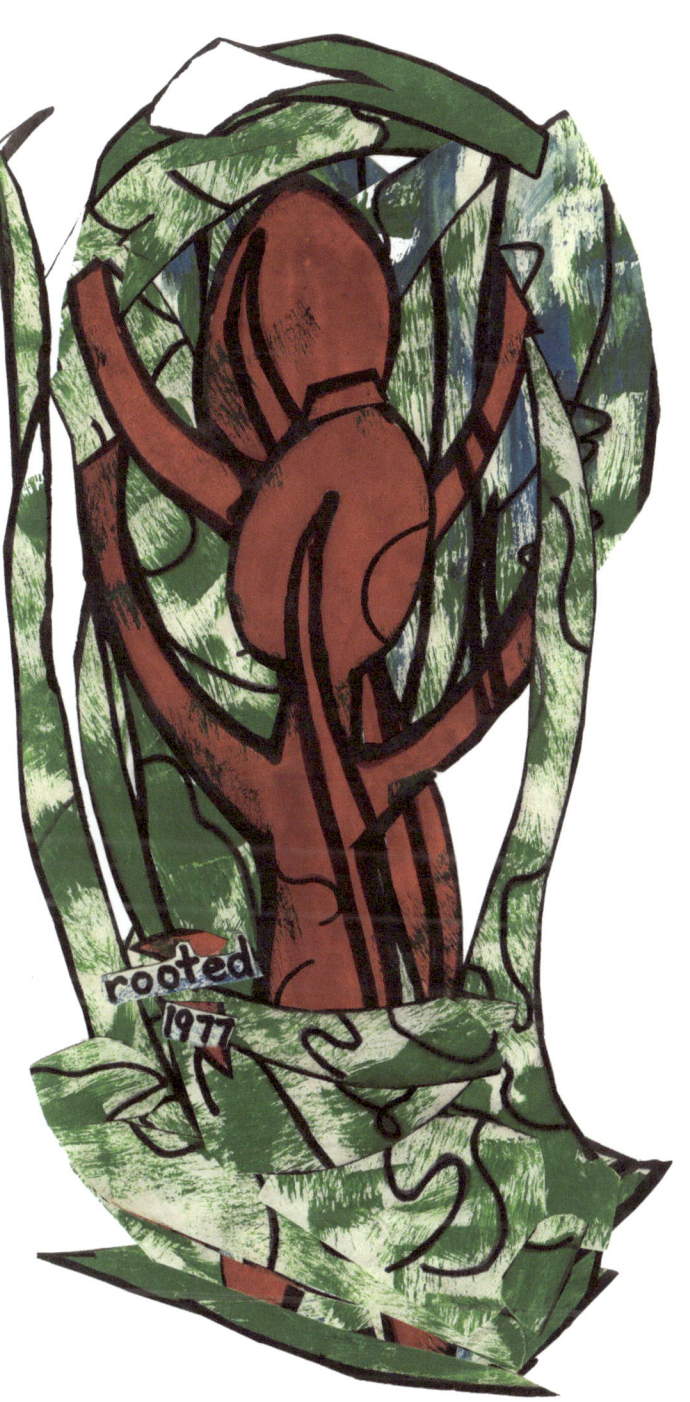

STRONGLY ROOTED

A tree lopsided against itself, Strongly Rooted resisted having her roots pulled up from under her. Hidden away in the forest she felt safe in amongst the trees where she spent most of her days unnoticed.

The true Gardener, though, had spotted her early on and arrived just in time to begin the process of chopping down her twisted, frail limbs that had grown wayworn with the years.

Not being ready for this kind of brutality, Strongly Rooted felt a surge of anger running through her, something like a blister that bursts open before it heals.

Unbeknownst to Strongly Rooted, a strange disease had inhabited the bark on her tree and because she only knew how to be one way in the forest, she could never receive help until the Gardener came.

At first, she disliked the Gardener and blamed him the way you would a pharmacist for giving you wrong medicine. Slowly the Gardener taught her that what she needed on a daily basis was an ounce of joy going into her bedraggled roots. The dose would be small at first but one day it would grow into something lavish.

As the bark on her tree became healthy and vibrant, Strongly Rooted gazed into the eyes of the Gardener and said, "I may have small branches but with You in me I've grown tall." "Indeed you have," said the Gardener and with that affirmation Strongly Rooted felt a new kind of Life Force gurgling in her.

Growing in small spurts and sometimes bigger spurts, her unconventional branches grew haphazardly in the air. Some branches shot up high while others hung down low. This was to accommodate an advanced breed of contemporary birds that found their way to her. As they nestled into the knobby branches of her twisted tree, their gnarled feathers made any kind of distortion appear beautiful.

Living inside the solid trunk of her tree, Strongly Rooted was definitely at home now in a forest that was so much vaster than she was. No longer lost or abandoned she attributed her success to the gracious Gardener.

Turning toward him, she said: "If you took an X-ray of the old me and the new me, every tree in the forest would bow down before you knowing that Love is the name of the only Gardener worth following."

GIFTED ORPHAN

Hoarding
the riches of God
is enough
to push anyone
down the stairs.

Losing your balance
you fall down
not up
and then
the drooling for Love
begins.

Take a ball now
bounce it higher
up over the head
of your orphaned self.

Spin the Energy forward
turn it upward
downward
inward
outward
let it be imprinted
on you.

Let go
of the limp cane
you carry
and see it
leap for joy.

GIFTED ORPHAN

"Life is like a cookbook," said Gifted Orphan. "It can be overwhelming at times. Too many recipes to choose from and you get lost in the mix." Confused by the menu, Gifted Orphan felt others were learning at a speed she could never keep up with.

Right from the start, she was a peculiar soul whose mind often drifted into a black hole on the left side of her brain, the analytical side that withheld the light from her. Anyone staring at her would have seen that the look on her face was vacant, as vacant as the interior space her body occupied.

Earth born teachers were accustomed to having students respond to the norm and so when it came to Gifted Orphan's quirky mannerisms they began asking: "Was she intelligent or was she not? And did she have a brain that was equipped to handle the now world in which she lived?"

As much as Gifted Orphan wanted to claim some form of intelligence, she became despondent and would brood over her dilemma for days, weeks, months and sometimes years at a time. Being different was not something she liked and embarrassment had a way of making her cheeks turn red.

In her silent spaces, though, when no one was watching, Gifted Orphan always knew who she was. There was a spiritual intensity in her that frightened some people away and drew others close.

One day when she was older, and less critical of herself, a woman with dark brown eyes moved away from the crowd of left brain thinkers and approached Gifted Orphan in a nonchalant way. Her energy was strong and she spoke with authority saying, "You know me." Gifted Orphan instantly felt at home. This time it wasn't about being smart or stupid but it had everything to do with intuitive wisdom.

Together, these women set up a restaurant where everyone was welcome. Left brain thinkers, right brain thinkers, everyone was accepted for who and what they were. In the middle of the menu were the words "Infinite Intelligence has drawn us together to love and be loved." The gifts grew and were rampant and everyone learned from one another.

There was an oasis here large enough to quench anyone on the outskirts of society who wanted to find their way in.

FREE SPIRIT

If you think
holes in an umbrella
can stop the rain
from coming through
you're resisting something.

Duplicity maybe
or ignorance
where the wet mouse
goes on pretending
that she's dry.

Stop
this game playing
turn your eyes inward
under the parched skin
of your body.

And say
to your thermometer:
if I could take
your temperature now
you'd have to admit
God is the abyss
you are falling into.

Like her
love her
be drawn to her
as the only magnet
left living for.

FREE SPIRIT

Free Spirit stood on top of a mountain, a new one she had never seen before. Feeling a fresh current of air swirling around her, this time she knew not to presume anything. Experience had taught her that as exhilarating as it is to stand on the peak of something majestic, it can often be the precursor to a person's downfall. In the case of Free Spirit, it was just that.

Innocently, she would keep going through the door of ignorance and allow herself to be lifted in an upward current to the summit of her dreams. Then losing her footing she would be hurled back down into a mundane world which is the place where most humans live.

Sometimes Free Spirit compared her journey to a see-saw. Up down. Down up. There were only two motions in it. Simple as it seemed, it was enough to give anyone nausea if repeated often enough.

In many ways, Free Spirit was an advanced learner hungering for a spirituality that was often beyond her grasp. Being immersed in a secular world, she could easily have lost her way and sometimes did.

On one occasion her see-saw experience ended up with a glitch. Instead of going up down, down up, it went down, down, down, into a remote land where devastation became her teacher.

This time Free Spirit's voice was barely audible and when it was heard, she said, "Sometimes it takes years, even centuries, for a volcano to erupt." Swallowing her pride, Free Spirit knew it was that kind of a mountain she was standing on and if anyone could teach her anything, this hot lava would.

Even though this experience was enough to crush her, it was also the moment of her own glorious breakthrough. Ethereal beings from the heavens descended on her and spoke more eloquently than any earth creatures ever had. "The Divine Potter needs a soul like yours," they said, "not puffed up because of success but flattened because of failure."

With that, their wings were broad enough to raise her up and whisk her away with a scoop of Infinity in it. Still living on the earth plane, Free Spirit felt the Life Force in her, a new kind of soul Energy that would change her life forever.

CLOSED MOUTH OPEN

Sometimes
calamity means
bumping into God
the wrong way.

That's when
erosion of the mind
sets in
and tells you:
that burnt out socket
in the light bulb
is you.

Imagine yourself now
wired differently
plugged into God
where you
and the radar
are one.

Slipping through
the portal
of God's mouth
there are
no words now
and, yet,
you revere everything!

You talk
without talking!

CLOSED MOUTH OPEN

One day God said to Closed Mouth Open, "Who are you when others push ahead of you to be first in line and does your name have anonymity attached to it?" Having never been challenged in this way, Closed Mouth Open looked at God despairingly and said, "I am nobody even though you have created me to be somebody."

Feeling somewhat squeamish and uncomfortable in God's presence, Closed Mouth Open knelt down and hid her face in the sand. "Oh," said God, "you're taking the easy way out which will only get you into more trouble."

This time there was an urgency in God's voice that came across as a reprimand. "Wake up," God said, "and stop this lethargic behaviour. You are older now and it's up to you to launch your own boat."

"Oh," said Closed Mouth Open, with her lips tightly sealed, "can the river of life really flow through me when I am nothing more than a trail of dust blowing in the wind?"

After a short lull in the conversation, God spoke up again. "Unless you move forward, your dead feet will remain stuck in the sand. Take up your oars and row your boat to where the ocean gives way to the sea."

This was all it took to have Closed Mouth Open launch out into the deeper waters. Sometimes she was deaf and blind to what lay ahead but already the beauty of God had captured her and she was ready to go wherever the destiny of her soul would lead.

From here on in, she never compared herself to others again. She was as free as she could ever be and fear, the enemy that had curtailed her, took a back seat in her boat. This time God rested at the helm and took Closed Mouth Open to where she needed to go.

Sometimes the waves and turbulent waters overtook her but having faith in her steersman always landed her on the new shore she was meant to climb.

Travelling through uncharted waters, Closed Mouth Open let go of her past, forgetting all the mistakes and follies that had at one time diminished her.

Moving forward with a fresh, new look on life, she let God's Spirit take hold of the mast in her sail and together they travelled freely with the wind at their back.

VICTORY

Standing in the ashes
of your burnt up self
you cannot postpone
your growth any longer.

You are too young
to become old again
and, yet,
if you choose darkness
instead of a lit lantern
it will burn you some more.

Only a survivor
can follow the trail
of black smoke
to where
the vision leads.

Unbeknownst to you
God could be out there
ticking like a clock
in the trees.

When the time comes
for you to rekindle
your flame
the burning will be over.

Out of the charred earth
you will rise up green again
even the twigs in the forest
know that.

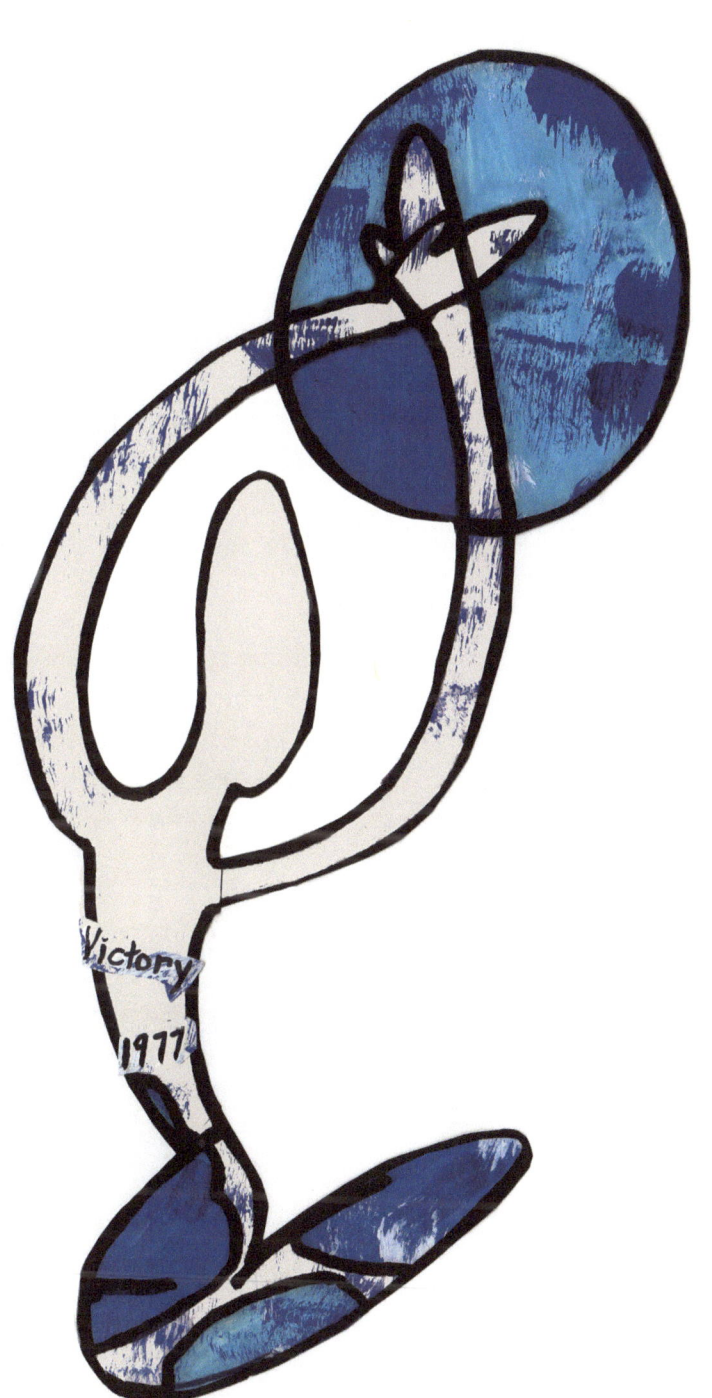

VICTORY

Victory and defeat lived on the same street and even though they bumped into one another often, it was only when defeat became an old woman that she eventually took the lead.

In their earlier years, they sometimes exchanged names. Victory became defeat and defeat became Victory. At first, nothing could stop these two from wrapping their arms around each other. It was a love affair with life that began when they were babies.

Early on, Victory chose to have her name begin with a capital letter and defeat, who was smaller in size, chose to have the lower case. Initially, each thought the other was important and, so, they got along well until the day when Victory grew older.

On that day, Victory, who represented the smart part of the population, tied her shoes instantly, but defeat, the smaller one in size, was slow at everything she did. Whether it was learning the alphabet or counting numbers, there was a tendency within her to freeze and whatever knowledge she had accumulated would come out backwards.

This made defeat hang her head in shame and go into a black zone, a disgruntled place that left her feeling empty. As much as defeat wanted to be a winner, someone who would get the gold certificate for coming first, the tendency to be a loser was what always overtook her.

Even though defeat had wonderful parents who loved her, defeat never loved herself. Unknowingly, she would keep God at a distance too, saying, "I love you and talk to you but where are you? Do you live in a refrigerator because all I get is a cold response when I approach you?"

One day when defeat's defences were down and she couldn't stand the chill any longer, God broke through the icy layers of her frigidity. Everything melted within and all around her. This time defeat knew she was loved and really loved.

Wherever she went from then on, defeat became Victory and together they were married into a lifelong commitment that had begun at their birth but was only now in old age being fully realized.

Placing a white robe on them, Divinity raised up defeat and Victory and together they celebrated that they were both winners.

DOORWAY THROUGH

Like God
joy is elusive.
Put her in the bath tub
and she'll bubble up
through the drain.

Place her in water
and she'll float past you
in a night time dream.
Put a lid on her
and she'll pop up naked
at your door.

With or without skin
if you think
life is permanent
she'll put a hole
in the ground
sitting under you.

At the end of day
put joy on a boat
in the river
and she'll paddle
her way home.

God and she are one
the glorious stream
of life
you can't put
a damper on.

DOORWAY THROUGH

When Doorway Through was young and innocent, she found it easy to say, "Joy is a white kite blowing in the wind. She is my playmate, the rainbow in my sky. Up, up she goes until I can see her no more."

Even at this young age, Doorway Through soon learned about the trickster in her. "Was it the face of God, or her own prickly face," she would ask, that had a way of always getting her in trouble.

Already trying to grasp the meaning of life, she would be mulling it over. "What is better," she would ask, "being good to yourself or being good to others," and as hard as she tried she could never come up with the right answer.

One day God snuck into her room and put a mirror on the wall. "Look at your face," God said, "and the answer will come to you." Somewhat surprised by the kind gesture of God, she heard the voice in her face say, "All it takes is a few too many heart breaks to have your innocence marred forever."

From then on, Doorway Through knew she was on good terms with God. If anyone was intelligent she knew that He was. On difficult days when the weather became too inclement for her to fly her kite, she would say, "What's up, God?" and then Father God would inform her that this time she needed to talk to Mother God who always knew from the beginning of time how to nurture souls in distress.

Years later in her journey when the fog got too thick for her to see, Doorway Through felt abandoned by both Father and Mother God. It was then that the Son appeared. His name was Jesus. "Come to me," Jesus said, "and I will restore you," and restore her He did.

Looking at her appearance, Jesus said, "You're not as uncomely to look at as you think. Remember me and the way I did it. You can do it too." Feeling reassured, Doorway Through let Jesus turn the knob on her door and as it opened, she got carried out of her small world into something more spacious.

The whole sky became illuminated with a bright light and Holy Spirit spoke to her through the cloud of unknowing. From then on, Doorway Through got led to her destination and together with Holy Spirit they entered the greatest of the great Lights.

FACE OF GOD

"Who are you hiding from?"
said the torn cloth
ripped open.
"No one," came the answer.
"I am the twisted one
made whole."

"Each time
I push back Infinity
she comes bursting
through my door."

"Scrape your skin open,"
she says,
"and the blood on my face
will be etched on yours."

"Touch me, feel me,
know me.
I am the invisible One
made visible."

"Woven into you now
I am the tapestry
of God's face
on your face
on everyone's face!"

"I am the script
of humanity
making herself known!"

Photo Acknowledgement: Saren K. Casad

FACE OF GOD

"Face of God, I am who I am," said the Voice coming toward me. "Know me as the I am One infusing love into every particle of your being. I cannot be something who I am not, so if I find you asleep, curled up under the covers, I will awaken you."

"Get up!" I will say. "You must feel Me to know Me. Like a river of blood, I cannot bear to see you bathed in it, and yet, it is the Life Force flowing through you and the whole of humanity that must be washed clean."

"If you look at the writing on the wall, you will see my Face inscribed on it. I am Jesus, Allah, Buddha. I am the God of all religions collapsing that which is divisive in them. I am Face of God, the Infinite One, and the ink in my pen is indelible."

"Even if the planet should destroy itself and the people on it, I will create a new tapestry and break open the hardened skin of the old. I will say to the capillaries in your body, wake up, bleed some more, and this time you will know that I am coming!"

"The veins and arteries in your body will acknowledge my Presence. They will spurt blood on the day of your birth, and you will know that I am here. You will bow down and I will raise you up. I am your God, the birth mother of you and the cosmos."

"Once you have seen Me, should anyone pluck out your eyes, you will no longer be standing in the dark. To have seen Me is to know Me and to know Me is to love Me."

"If you or anyone else desires it, you could be the new Mary Magdalene's walking on the face of the earth or the Virgin herself, bringing the Jesus of Nazareth back to life in a garb where this time everyone would know him."

"If you listen to Me, you will know that the I am who I am Face of God has spoken. And should your ears be deafened by the thunder of my speech, you could still be heralding in the second coming of the Christ without your knowing it. Horrible as it may be, the purging of innocent young children, women and men in your time could be the very blood that will destroy and awaken you."

"In the dark eye of your blindness, you could be covering Me over and still I will be sprouting up in your midst. Yesterday, today and tomorrow will slip away, but I will not slip away."

Eileen Curteis, ssa

Photograph by
Frances Litman
www.franceslitman.com

ABOUT THE AUTHOR

For the last 26 years, Eileen Curteis, a Sister of Saint Ann, has been involved in the Reiki Healing Ministry, a revered eastern healing art that she combines with her Christian heritage of healing. A former teacher, principal and educator for 27 years, Eileen shares that her greatest passion now lies in her healing ministry and in the literary arts. She has authored twelve books to date and has become an accomplished poet, artist, and writer, as well as being a producer of seven CDs and three films. She lives in Victoria, BC.

You can view Eileen's books, CDs, and DVDs at: www.BooksofExcellence.com

www.ingramcontent.com/pod-product-compliance
Lightning Source LLC
Chambersburg PA
CBHW041432300426
44117CB00001B/2